D1202820

FEAR
IS MY CO-PILOT

ADVANCE PRAISE

In *Fear Is My Co-Pilot*, Don Wooldridge does a wonderful job of taking us through his journey of finding out about his diagnosis, the impact his symptoms have on his relationships and jobs, and how he learned what works best for him to manage his symptoms. As you will see in reading his story, this was a journey decades in the making.

Don's insights are beautifully illustrated through his own experiences. He finds both the advantages and disadvantages of his symptoms, noting what an amazing creative problem-solver he can be . . . at the very peaks of his hypomanic episodes, but then addresses the effects that drive can have on those around him.

~ Krylyn Peters
The Fear Whisperer is a licensed psychotherapist, an author, speaker, coach, and singer/songwriter.
www.krylyn.com

Fear Is My Co-Pilot was a riveting read; it was at times heart- rending, disquieting, and funny. Wooldridge's articulate, lightly filtered memoir is a captivating glimpse into a turbulent mind.

~Therese Skelly
Licensed Therapist, Money/Mindset Mentor, Business Catalyst, and Transformational Teacher.
http://happyinbusiness.com/

We must accept finite disappointment, but

never lose infinite hope.

Martin Luther King, Jr. (1929-1968)
American Baptist minister, activist, humanitarian, and leader in
the African-American Civil Rights Movement.

FEAR
IS MY CO-PILOT

My Bipolar II Journey

by

Don Wooldridge

Copyright ©2016 by Don Wooldridge. All Rights Reserved.

D & PW Publishing, Phoenix, Arizona
ISBN-13: 978-0692606773
ISBN-10: 0692606777

All rights reserved. No part of this book may be used or reproduced by any means, graphic, electronic, or mechanical, including photocopying, recording, taping or by any information storage retrieval system without the written permission of the author.

Requests to the Publisher for permission should be addressed to

DP& PW Publishing 215 N Power Rd, # 428 Mesa, AZ 85205-8455.

Limit of Liability Disclaimer of Warranty. While the Publisher and author have used their best efforts in preparing this book, they make no representations or warranties with respect to the accuracy or completeness of this book and specifically disclaim any implied warranties of merchantability or fitness for a particular purpose. No warranty may be created or extended by sales representatives or written sales materials. The publisher and author are not engaged in rendering professional services, and you should consult with a professional where appropriate. Neither publisher nor author shall be liable for any loss or profit or other commercial damages, including but not limited to special, incidental, consequential or other damages.

For general information on other books written by this author contact DP& PW Publishing 215 N Power Rd, # 428 Mesa, AZ 85205-8455.

Printed in the United States of America

10 9 8 7 6 5 4 3 2 1

Cover design by... Patrick Sipperly

DEDICATION

This book is dedicated to each reader who dreams of reducing their suffering of Bipolar Type II disorder, or that of someone whom they love. It is my hope and dream that this book might be the first step; that my story will help another person successfully manage their Bipolar II disorder.

TABLE OF CONTENTS

SECTION III

FOREWORD

In *Fear is My Copilot* Don Wooldridge writes about his experiences with Bipolar disorder and how he lived a productive life based on the lessons that he learned along the way as a result of those experiences. This book draws upon Don's personal experiences—to help each reader understand the disorder, how to manage it over the long-term, and how to support those who suffer from this debilitating condition.

The word "Bipolar" refers to the two extremes of mood: depression and mania. Early on, the term "manic depression" was also used. Bipolar disorder is a life-long condition that affects every aspect of your life. It's difficult to imagine the havoc a condition known as Bipolar disorder can wreak on an individual's life, as well as those around them.

While each person's experience is unique and there is a continuum between extreme moods and the normal mood swings that most everyone experiences, if you suffer from Bipolar disorder, you know the significant impact on your life, and can even put your life at risk. Despite its life-long existence, you can go on to live a productive life once you receive proper treatment, gain empowering knowledge, employ viable self-management strategies, and maintain good levels of social support. These interventions can make you feel like you're making progress each day.

This book is indeed timely for two reasons. First, mental health practitioners have recently begun to appreciate that the symptoms and functional deficits of Bipolar disorder involve a great deal more than mood, so are enlarging their focus. Second, there are still many unanswered questions about this condition, so when individuals share their experiences, it provides valuable information for researchers and clinicians alike to make more useful contributions to the mental health field.

I feel a special affinity for the topic of mental illness, because not only am I a psychologist, I also have first-hand experience with clinical depression. And according to the World Health Organization, it is a major health problem around the world that affects people of all socioeconomic and educational levels. Recovery is a life-long journey that is unique to each individual. A certain gratitude for the little things is what you will read in Don's book; similarly, I am grateful to have lived a vibrant and productive life for many years now since my diagnosis in the early-1980s.

Despite considerable attention that has recently been drawn to mental illness and rapid progress in the research and treatment of Bipolar disorder, mental illness in general still carries a social stigma. One of my life missions is to chip away at this stigma. My hope is that after reading this book you will have acquired more knowledge about this debilitating disorder and will have a greater understanding of and compassion for those who suffer from this common, but somewhat neglected condition.

~ **Mary Canty Merrill, PhD**
President & COO
Industrial/Organizational Psychologist
http://merrillca.com/

AUTHOR'S NOTES

———— ✦ ————

BIPOLAR DISORDER IS a chronic illness with no cure ...

The causes of Bipolar disorder point to instability in the transmission of nerve impulses in the brain, which is related to the brain's biochemistry; the tendency toward mood instability is considered to be genetically transmitted. [1]

People with Bipolar disorder experience drastic shifts in mood, energy, thoughts, behavior, and the ability to function that are out of proportion or unrelated to their environments.[2]

Bipolar I disorder is considered the more classic form of the disease. It is marked by recurrent episodes of mania and

---

[1] Bipolar 101, A Practical Guide;2009 Ruth C. White, PH.D.,MPH,MSW and John D. Preston, PSY.D., ABPP

[2] Bipolar 101, A Practical Guide;2009 Ruth C. White, PH.D.,MPH,MSW and John D. Preston, PSY.D., ABPP

depression with possible mixed episodes.[3] Bipolar II disorder is marked by milder episodes of hypomania which subtly alternates with depression, but without full manic episodes.

———— • ————

BEFORE YOU FOLLOW my story through these pages, I think a "Heads Up!" is in order.

My life journey with Bipolar II disorder involved intense emotional reactions, unpredictability, and repetition of unhealthy symptoms and behaviors. In many ways, I never quite knew where I was heading next.

I kept my psychological disorder closeted for 35 years. Even though my parents and sisters learned about it at its onset in 1973, the topic never graced our conversations again until I was in my sixties. Only after writing an autobiography for my children in 2009 did I disclose my disorder to them. Before my robotic heart procedure in 2008, I shared my Bipolar disorder with four of my closest friends. Since my diagnosis in

---

[3] Bipolar 101, A PracticalGuide;2009   Ruth C. White, PH.D.,MPH,MSW and John D. Preston, PSY.D., ABPP

1973, only eleven people are aware of it, seven of whom are family.

Mine has been a life filled with a fear of discovery; the Bipolar disorder affected my family, friends, and work numerous times. Each event consequently caused me enormous anxiety, distress, remorse, and guilt. It would have been easy to blame my behavior on my mental disorder, but I refused to expose myself, for fear of what people would say or do after the discovery.

Not wanting this book to mirror the *wanderings of a psychological disorder,* I have chosen to reveal my lessons learned about living with Bipolar II in the sequence, and the years the events occurred.

This chronological flow for the story makes more sense to me, because I want to share the symptoms with you before I reveal the discoveries. It's the myriad discoveries along my journey that became the building blocks for managing Bipolar II disorder.

I write with much difficulty about private events and emotions; much like stepping onto the town square naked. I feel a need to tell my story, and what kept me alive, even when death attempted to seduce me. I choose to share my personal history, because no matter how painful the recall has been—this disease thrives in a world of silence.

I want to be a part of those who shatter this silence, and share ways to live well with Bipolar disorders. But first, we must understand our enemy... a slumbering serpent that strikes unexpectedly and takes over our lives.

Prior to my diagnosis I had heard co-workers talking about people who were mentally ill in a cruel, judgmental, demeaning and dismissive way. Their behavior served to increase my fear of discovery after I was diagnosed as manic-depressive, which caused me to withdrew into myself even more. I vowed that there was no way anyone was going to talk about me that way. I had to protect my job, my home and my family. My illness became my secret life, hidden from view, deep inside me.

Throughout a forty-year journey I learned so much, yet still could never change my condition. Perhaps you'll find the lessons I've learned on my journey helpful.

All poetry written by the author may not be used without his written consent.

DISCLAIMER

THIS MEMOIR IS not intended in any way to dispense medical advice concerning any Bipolar or manic-depressive condition or the medications used to treat them.

All comments, conditions, feelings, attitudes, and behaviors described herein are based solely on the personal experiences of the author. All things learned or described during interactions with the author's doctors are not exact quotations, but paraphrased from memory, as best recalled.

To diagnose or treat any Bipolar disorder, you must seek out the advice of a medical professional. Only through a qualified diagnosis by a psychiatrist, and subsequent therapy, will you be able to understand the extent of your illness and the medications and treatment required to stabilize the illness.

SECTION I

THE 1970'S

CONFLICT

1971

Inside my shell it feels like hell,
And my soul is dying.[1]

THE PRICE I *pay for the success on my job means so little at home. How is it I am a superstar at work and a misfit at home?*

Gone were the days of romance, like our moonlight engagement in the Chinese Gardens of San Antonio, Texas. Gone were the days of joy and adventure as we survived my last two years of college. What we were left with was to put on our public faces and pretend to be a happy, healthy married couple. Away from home we behaved like we were peaches and cream.

The more this occurred the more confused I became. If she loved me, why did she treat me this way? I continued to withdraw into myself.

---

[1] ©Don Wooldridge

The public peaches and cream routine never lasted long; as soon as we were alone, I'd hear criticism, condemnation, and complaints about my behavior. According to the one who was supposed to love me, even my style of dress wasn't appropriate. I remember one evening, getting ready to go out, and my wife stood looking at me as I descended the stairs in tennis shoes and a polo shirt. Often times she'd disapprove of what I chose to wear. I might have a plaid shirt on when she thought it should be striped. I'd dress casual when she thought I should wear a sport coat. Just silly stuff to me, actually, but this time she ordered me to go back upstairs and change, making me feel just like a kid.

Often these conversations turned into an argument, fused with deep anger, but in my thoughts, I tried to manage the potentially destructive emotions, *In the end it's just easier to do what she says than to deal with the conflict all night!* Her constant disapproval made me feel like I didn't even fit in my own home. I could never relax and feel comfortable; I knew at any moment I could do something my wife thought wrong. There was constant tension and conflict between us. We grew apart.

The stress of my management responsibility at work, two children under six, and the disapproval from my wife became overwhelming. I began a span of erratic behavior that affected my decisions, threatened to terminate my career, and in the end, forever altered my future.

Confused, I couldn't understand why there was such a big difference between the way I was treated at work and at home. As we made our way through 1971, I resented the pretending that went on when my wife and I were out together with friends; I ultimately could see no way to change the situation other than separating.

I moved downtown into the only cheap apartment I could afford. Surrounded by drunks, derelicts, and possibly hookers, I lived in a dark and dull apartment among the night people. It felt wonderful. I was relieved of the tension and torment I'd felt living at home. My depression lifted, letting me feel in control of myself for a little while.

I didn't have much money and no social life to speak of. Alone, except for my job and co-workers, all of my feelings were temporary. I'd have days of brightness followed by gloomy days of self-analysis, despair, and confusion. Suicidal thoughts were frequent when I felt trapped in a corner, thrust there by the lack of money, contentious visitations, or conflict with my wife. Once entrapped within that mood, suicide rolled over and over in my mind.

With no one to talk to, I would write to express my innermost feelings. It seems ridiculous, because I was not a writer and didn't even read poetry at the time. But, somehow my thoughts spilled out on paper in rhyme.

Going Sailing

Inside my shell I feel like hell,
and my soul is dying.

As I contemplate life, death,
laughing and crying.

From day to day feelings vary,
and are mostly temporary.

But I wrestle with life, wondering why
people would rather live than die.

Is death like being drunk?
Slowly failing, lightly sailing,
Kneeling to the ground with a thump!

Death doesn't seem that bad to me.
I think that's where I want to be.

So tonight, I'll watch my life failing,
as I go lightly sailing.

©Don Wooldridge

Living alone was not fun at all. Tensions from home may have been erased, but I discovered there was no way to escape my fear. Keeping our separation quiet from those at work, and my Bipolar illness, it felt like I was leading a double life that could never blend together. As a result, I thought if this was the life I could expect as a result, it would be ridiculous.

I wondered, *What price will I pay to coexist with her? What price am I willing to I pay to stay with my two young boys?*

There had to be some way to do this without living in squalor. After three months of separation, I returned home to my wife and family, determined to try again. Although my wife welcomed me back, there was a price to pay. She was increasingly suspicious, and although I never thought it possible, even more controlling. Though we were living together again, our marriage continued to be tense, at best.

STRESS

1972

—————◆—————

I WAS VERY successful working for John Deere's Industrial Equipment Division in Dubuque, Iowa. Each year the company transferred or promoted me into a different job. I started as an engineering draftsman, then was promoted to service publications during my second year there, and personnel employment representative later on. Working in the personnel department in 1970, I noticed repeated terminations in the service training department, and discussed the issue with my boss, the personnel manager. I complained about having to continually hire new employees for a manager with the worst turnover rate in our factory of 8,000 employees. During our discussion I boldly told him, "I can do a better job managing this department!" Although he agreed a problem existed, he didn't respond to my remark.

A few months later my boss called me into his office and announced he had good news regarding the service training department. He was promoting me to be the new service training manager. I was both shocked and excited. That is, until I heard "the rest of the story."

The service department manager had reservations about me being technically qualified to do the job, and wanted me to work for six months to learn the business and prove myself. The caveat? No one could know I would become the new manager, or the deal was off. In essence, they expected me to work under deep cover for six months, alongside the man they expected me to replace, and the employees I would eventually supervise. My salary would not change until they terminated the current department manager.

I accepted the challenge, convinced I could do a better job. Plus my industrial arts education degree fit the service training function perfectly. All I had to do was deal with the stress . . . which started on day one.

Walking into the service training department, I am hit with questions from everyone—fellow employees and the department manager. My body reacts to the stress in much the same way I'd feel walking off the beach into an ocean of waves that would knock me down every time I'd get up. I fight against the swell of questions and make up answers as fast as I can.

The department manager I was picked to replace asked, "What makes you qualified to work here? You don't have any service experience."

Co-workers asked, "Did you work at a dealership? Where did you service construction equipment? Why are you here?"

10

Of course, I received the dirtiest, nastiest, and toughest jobs, just to test me, and it seemed everyone set out to make me prove myself—every hour of every day.

Thank God I'm a quick learner.

I relied on all my youthful experiences working for my dad. As a teenager I'd been a mechanic's helper on mining and quarry equipment. Dad insisted I rebuild a V-8 engine one summer, so I could become familiar and very comfortable working with tools. Beyond assessing my skills, my fellow trainers at John Deere were looking over my shoulder, and the department manager appeared to be stalking me. Shortly thereafter I realized my co-workers had withheld information from me; I resorted to stealth to find one person in the factory with the information I needed to do my job.

In the service training classroom I had to teach the most undesirable topics, one of which was the charging system in our machines. Previously the instructors had taught the internal schematic of the regulator, how it worked and regulated electrical power. Of course, they expected me to learn, teach, and know all the details about this regulator. First of all, there wasn't time to do that, and my mistrustful manager knew this. It soon became quite obvious he expected me to fail. However, I found that the new regulator was now sealed, solid state, and a throw-away component if it malfunctioned. We no longer needed to know the internal operation!

Quickly, I deleted the bulk of the lesson plan, except for the test instrument and the testing process. Basically the test results would be "Go" or "No-Go."

As my classes begin, a co-worker or my manager sits in to observe and evaluate me. My nerves are on edge, being aware they are always looking for ways to get rid of me. It's not going to happen in this classroom!

I have always known I am most comfortable in a classroom. So, unlike their previous lecture techniques, I included shop exercises and facilitate stimulating participation; I encouraged questions, and answered them successfully. My regulator lesson was clear, simple, and realistic.

Feedback from participants was very positive, and caused my co-workers to question what they had been doing, and found themselves willing to step up their game to be more like me. The department manager played down my success as luck. However, over time I quelled the tsunami and calmed the rocky waters to only whitecaps.

Still, it feels like life or death!

I not only worried about lasting six months, but questioned if I even wanted to supervise this backward, dysfunctional department.

Work was on my mind constantly, not to mention the intense focus I tried to maintain within myself to keep the secret about my role in the service training department.

The pressure was rather like a boiling pot, with new thoughts bubbling up. I continually thought about what might happen next. My mind buzzed as I continually role-played possible situations, and how to handle them. The questions… always the questions: What should I say? What should I do? Who can I trust?

At home my wife expected me to fit in and be normal; her repeated recriminations caused even more tension within and created feelings that came out as my being moody, defensive, and volatile. Without any encouraging words from her, the personnel manager, or the service manager, I felt like I didn't exist in anyone's world. I became stubborn and defensive because I'd boldly proclaimed I could do a better job, and I had to prove it!

Eventually it felt like I was carrying a bomb on my back, and if anyone noticed, it would explode. I could only have guarded conversations with fellow employees. Confusion, anger, misery . . . *I am beginning to feel exhausted from the constant fear I will make the one big mistake that will blow the whole thing.*

How could I possibly have known what I was doing to myself? Many years later I learned that psychological science has proven stress has a definite and direct impact on brain functions.

"Stress raises the levels of steroid hormones in the bloodstream, and cortisol, the most important of these hormones, is practically toxic to neurons in the most important mood-regulation center of the brain, the hippocampus." [4]

It also appears that the impact of stress on people's brain health is affected by other behaviors that can also harm the brain. Overeating, drinking alcohol and smoking cigarettes are among the informal stress management approaches people employ, but all of them increase the risk of damage to the brain in the form of a stroke.

The stress hormone, known as cortisol, is public-health-enemy number one. Scientists have categorically accepted for years that elevated cortisol levels: interfere with learning and memory, lower immune function and bone density, increase weight gain, blood pressure, cholesterol, heart disease... the list goes on and on.

Chronic stress and elevated cortisol levels also increase risk for depression, and lower life expectancy. [5]

---

[4] Psychology Today, Cortisol: Why "The Stress Hormone" Is Public Enemy No.1

[5] Psychology Today, Cortisol: Why "The Stress Hormone" Is Public Enemy No.1

Let me repeat, the steroid hormone called cortisol destroys neuron cells in the mood center of the brain. As I think back to this period of time, under the highest stress of my life, I realize just how destructive stress was to my mental health.

When the rigors of the six months finally ended, the department manager was fired. The company promoted me, as promised; my fellow trainers were shocked. They were surprised to learn that I had been listening to them, and as a result were more than satisfied to see so many of their ideas implemented as I reorganized the department, changed the curriculum, and changed procedures.

With the cloak of secrecy lifted, my attitude changed from fear and depression to hypomania. A flood of responsibility and information rained down on me. I loved the creative problem-solving that was required, and the results were exciting as our dealer organization gave us, and the service manager, positive feedback about the changes in the service training department.

My success as a department manager opened the way to one of the most exciting and challenging assignments I could imagine. In 1972 I was asked to research and design an industrial equipment training center for our worldwide service personnel. I traveled for ten or twelve months throughout the United States, visiting the elite training centers of large corporations like Xerox, Marriott, and Caterpillar. I had ideas galore and visions in my head that ended up as strategic plans and a facility design. At the end of the year, these plans were finally reviewed by our factory's top management staff. I was more than elated when they accepted the plan and then sent on to the John Deere Corporate Headquarters.

Alas! The joy was not to be a constant in my life, and when the actual creation/building of the training center was postponed for five years, all the "air" went out of me... leaving me feeling as flat as a punctured balloon.

Now I feel betrayed. No, I am more than that; I am mad, despondent, and depressed. Does no one realize I put my heart and soul into this project and design?

Everyone complimented me on the results of my effort, agreeing it was an excellent plan. They couldn't understand the delay either. Senior managers consoled me, saying, "This is just how corporations work."

It was a serious blow to my ego.

I was devastated.

I never recovered... resulting in my hospitalization, and a diagnosis that changed the course of my life.

OUT OF MY WINDOW

1973

———◆———

A SQUIRREL PLAYING on a tree outside in the courtyard breaks my blank stare out of the hospital window.

I have no idea how long I've been staring out the window. I don't even remember coming to the psychiatric ward of this hospital. All I know is I'm in Dubuque, Iowa.

Sitting there, I struggled with my scattered thoughts, I pondered how it was only yesterday I was a successful middle manager for a Fortune 500 company.

What went wrong? Did someone bring me here, or did I just walk in myself seeking help?

Watching the squirrel play on the tree again, I found myself longingly wishing it were me, so I'd be out of here and free.

"Free" has been an important desire lately. I've felt so pressured, restrained. Even unwelcome in my own home.

As random thoughts rush through my mind I wonder, *am I depressed? Maybe suicidal? I know I've been angry with my wife—yelled, screamed, and shoved her around. But doesn't everybody go through that?*

The tapping sounds of a woman's heels echoing in the empty hallway broke my solitude. Turning to see who is approaching, my wife appeared—walking beside a man I didn't recognize. She had a smile on her face. Scooting to the center of my bed as they enter my sterile hospital room, I sighed.

This can't be good. Something is up.

"Don, we need to talk. Will you pay attention to me for a minute, please?" the psychiatrist asked.

"Okay."

"Your wife and I have talked about your condition and treatment options. I'd like to share that information with you. First of all, I've determined that you're suffering from a brain disorder called manic-depression."

What he just said didn't register, since my brain was still cloudy and sluggish. But I did hear him say, "brain disorder," and considering the stress in our relationship of late, I wondered if my wife convinced him of that.

"What does that mean?" I asked.

"What we know at this point in time is that this disorder causes severe mood swings, like a roller coaster. A few years ago doctors lumped it in with schizophrenia, and unfortunately patients were housed in mental institutions for a lifetime to separate them from society. We've come a long way since then, realizing that manic-depression is not as severe as schizophrenia and can be treated with medication and therapy."

"Holy cow! A mental institution?"

"No, Don. You're not going to a mental institution," he said. "We can treat your condition to reduce the impact of your mood swings. Your wife and I have discussed a treatment plan that will involve electroshock in hopes of reviving brain functions that are not working as well as they should."

As I began to comprehend what the doctor said, I found it almost impossible to believe my wife ever agreed with the doctor to electroshock me.

Easy for her to say! Just watch them fry my brain! God, if I didn't like her before, I hate her now. What is she thinking?

"No! No! No!" Shaking my head vigorously I slide off the bed onto my feet. Standing up to him, much to my wife's surprise, I blurt out, "This is not the Middle Ages. I am signing nothing and I'm not having my brain shocked. What the hell will I be like afterward? Tell me that, will ya?"

19

My wife stepped between us, "Don, what do you think you're doing? This doctor is here to help you. Please, just sit down and listen. This is serious."

I don't know what the doctor thinks about this encounter, but he sure looks composed. Evidently he is used to people like me.

The doctor continued his assessment. "Don, the only other alternative is to try to treat your condition with medication. I can start you on a dosage of lithium carbonate, monitor your progress for the next few days, and if you respond well, I'll send you home."

"Fine, I'll do that instead." Shaking her head, my wife and the doctor left together, leaving me alone to stare out my window again.

Now I can't even concentrate. Random thoughts are floating through my head, spiraling me into a deep, dark mood. What is this? Why do I feel like I am caught in some kind of whirlpool? Why am I here?

These questions made clanging sounds in my head like a church bell on Sunday morning, and try as I might, I had no answers. At one time I worried about having a nervous breakdown, but really didn't know what that was, or where to go for help. We had never talked about it at home, so I was left thinking perhaps my doctor sent me here following a recent appointment.

It doesn't matter how it happened; it's just that I am in some emotional pit that I can't climb out of.

The spinning and swirling thoughts dissipated as I found my head clearing. An awareness came over me, recognizing that how I got here didn't matter to me as much as who would know about it. Almost immobilized by this new fear, questions stream through my mind.

Does everybody know about this? If people at work know, will this end my career? What will my family say when they find out? Has my wife told anybody? Everything I've worked for could be ruined if this isn't kept as a secret.

In the midst of all my confusion, one thing became very clear: I could never disclose the fact that I have a mental illness. Never! My questions are overshadowed by the knowledge that I have a brain disorder I can't explain or get rid of. Powerless, and facing a new fear, I wonder.

Is this illness going to define my life forever? Did I just catch it, or have I had it all my life?

WHEN DID THIS HAPPEN?

1973

———— • ————

IT'S HARD TO tell if I had this mental disorder as a child, but I do remember negative emotions disrupting my life the summer of 1962, just before my senior year of high school. Moodiness showed up, and my self-destructive reaction to stress soon followed.

I was a three-sport athlete at a school where athletics were extremely competitive. There were 4600 students when I started my sophomore year, and competition for a spot on any team was intense.

State championships were the goal every year. Our coaches were the best in the state of Iowa. The football program won nine state championships and the current coach, "Butch" Stolfa, played for the Chicago Bears. Our basketball program won seven championships and was coached by Harvey Schmidt, an All-American from the University of Illinois. The baseball program won 11 state championships

and was coached by Joe Lutz, a former catcher for the
St. Louis Browns.

I was a good baseball player, an all-star every year, and
one of the two best hitters on the high school team. My skills,
combined with coach Lutz's pro contacts, earned me a place
on a semi-pro team, so scouts could see me play against older
players. I was excited to play semi-pro ball because I wanted
to do anything for a chance to play in the major leagues.

I loved playing baseball, and during the summer I played
on the all-star team first, then when that game was over I'd
drive to the semi-pro diamond. I'd arrive about nine p.m. and
start the third inning of the game. At six the next morning,
with only five or six hours sleep, I was on my way to my
construction job.

Enthusiasm carried me, and it was fun at first. Then,
gradually, the schedule became grueling, and finally I felt the
effects of exhaustion. The stress of trying to perform
maximally at so many things caused me to burnout, and I quit
the semi-pro league.

My coach was furious. White Sox and Yankees scouts
were watching that league for minor league players, and I
blew it. He was so mad he hardly acknowledged me when I
was around him.

With summer over football season started. It was our
senior year and we were ready to erase the distasteful season
of last year. My friend Vern and I were co-captains. The team

was excited, but I wasn't prepared for what occurred to me after our loss to our competitor, Iowa City High School.

A close 14-12 score, we held the upper hand most of the game. Our defense was strong and held off Iowa City until late in the fourth quarter. Our defensive back let a receiver get behind him and catch a pass for a touchdown, which resulted in their win; our disappointment ran deep.

In spite of the loss, the highlight of playing Iowa City High School was our stop for dinner at a famous Amana Colonies restaurant. Lots of great food, served family style, meant we could "pig out" for free. But, it didn't feel like a highlight tonight. Seated across from each other at long tables players grumbled.

"This sucks! We had the game won," Tom Ryan said as he dug into a bowl of mashed potatoes.

Steve Sindt pounded his knife handle on the table, "Yeah, we whip their butts all night, and just one stinking play makes us losers. It's not right."

Of course I agreed, but there was no let up. Everyone around me was in a bad mood and negative. I was feeling claustrophobic and depressed, and suddenly felt I just couldn't take it anymore.

"I'm going to the rest room, guys." I said as I left our table. But, I didn't do that, instead I slipped outside to a quiet place where I could be alone with my own dark thoughts.

A little while later I was surprised when the door burst open behind me. Before I knew it coach Liddy was in front of me snarling into my face.

"Just what do you think you're doing?"

"I'm feeling really down, coach. I need a little time to myself."

"Oh, you do, do you. And you don't think your teammates are feeling down, too. I depend on you, Wooldridge. You were elected a co-captain because you're a leader, and this is exactly the time when I expect you to lead, not hide out alone in the dark. Now, if you want to be co-captain of this team you'd better get your butt in there and do what you can to help your teammates get over this loss. Now, go!"

Unfortunately, too depressed to help anybody, I put on my best show, just in case coach Liddy was watching. Co-captain or not, I had a problem understanding why all of a sudden I was in the bottom of a very dark barrel and immobilized. I'd never felt this way before.

I've frequently heard eighteen-year-olds can be as emotionally stable as a beach ball in the breeze. However, I don't remember my behavior quite that way. I was in the second year of dating the same girl, but our senior year together was volatile—mostly because of me. I would explode with anger at surprising and inappropriate times. There was no way for me to predict or recognize the stimulus causing it. I'd just explode.

I wasn't wise enough to put the pieces together and realize my behavior was changing. My moods were bounding like a ping pong ball. When baseball started the spring of my senior year coach Lutz was still mad at me. My moodiness just made the relationship worse.

Counting on me to perform as a sub, coach Lutz would put me in tight situations during a game. Unlike previous years as an all- star when I'd been exceptional, there were times now when I simply could not seem to deliver. This growing, yet still unfamiliar moodiness, would control me at the most inopportune times.

Beyond sports, there was constant conflict at home. My parent's expected me to go to college. The Russian Sputnik had landed on the moon and society felt that "all God's children must go to college." Personally, I had no idea where to go or what to study. Maybe business?

I was angry and confused as the school year neared its conclusion. My dream of playing baseball had died and I had been forced to make a decision about college. And, I hated the claustrophobic atmosphere of my father checking up on me every weekend. He'd call his buddies from businesses and church to learn what they may have heard about where I was, what I was doing, and who I was with, and then follow up to interrogate me and challenge my version of the reality.

I wanted the freedom to experiment and see what I might want out of life, not the cookie cutter expectations of my parents. Even my girlfriend had expectations, and I wasn't sure about meeting those either.

The continued growing feelings of hate, anger and claustrophobia drove me away from home. There were no good feelings there, and I had to get away to find some elsewhere.

Fueled by emotions, I escaped it all by going to college 2000 miles away in San Marcos, Texas.

It's a shame that I was so blind and bullheaded when I left high school. There were good things to be found at home; I was just temporarily blinded to them. A millwright I worked with for four years as a welder's helper, recognized my talent and offered me an apprenticeship when I graduated from high school.

Without a thorough understanding of the innate talent in metal working I was given by a heritage of Wooldridge blacksmiths going back centuries to Great Britain, my irrational and emotional decision to leave town led me to decline his offer. Having the opportunity to look back now, I wonder if age 18 was the beginning of my Bipolar condition. Would it have stayed dormant if I had accepted the apprenticeship and not gone to college?

LITHIUM

1973

———•———

WELL, IF MY Bipolar disorder was beginning to show itself in 1962, it's out of the bag now. I've refused Electroconvulsive Therapy (ECT) and chosen to try medications to lessen the impact of this illness.

Before I was released from the hospital my doctor and I discussed treating my mood disorder with medication.

"Don," he said, "There's a drug that has just recently been introduced (1973) called lithium. I'm going to prescribe three, 300 mg tablets, a day."

"900 mg of lithium a day? That seems like a lot." I said.

The doctor went on and explained the process. "Don, with this medication you'll need to have blood tests every three months to monitor the level of lithium in your system. You'll need to schedule the test twelve hours after taking your last dose. There's a therapeutic range of L-0.6 mEq/L to L-1.2mEq/L that we need to maintain in your blood stream for this drug to work properly."

I think I can do this! It seems a lot more practical than electro-shock.

"Also, Don," the doctor continued, "I don't want you to change your lifestyle or eating habits. Especially salt. I want you to maintain the same level of salt in your diet as you normally have done in the past."

"What's salt got to do with this?"

"Lithium is made up of salts. If your salt intake is reduced, the lithium level will decline also and possibly render it ineffective. Then again, too much could make you toxic. That's why you need to maintain the blood testing."

You might think a long-term dosage of this much salt would cause high blood pressure, but over the years it's never been a problem. My test results have never shown any issue, and the original dosage hasn't changed in over forty years. Given the choice between electroshock and pills, it was easy for me to embrace the routine of taking lithium.

Still traumatized by the shock of having a mental disorder I had no idea how lucky I had just become. Behind the scenes, the world of psychiatry was divided. You may think a doctor prescribing medication would be simple enough. After all, patients take medication for any number of reasons, including high blood pressure and diabetes.

"But in the 1970's, when lithium and other effective medications for "functional" illnesses came along, persons with Bipolar disorder and schizophrenia left therapists behind and made tracks for a new kind of doctor: the biological psychiatrist called a "pharmacotherapist." For a time there was a kind of schism in American psychiatry between those who believed that dynamic psychology best explained mental illnesses and those who believed that biology was the key that would unlock the mysteries of psychiatric disorders."[6]

Unknowingly, I was diagnosed and treated by a new breed pharmacotherapist.

There are adverse effects using Lithium carbonate. It can damage the thyroid, kidneys, and liver. Whenever my doctors ordered my blood tests, they included the testing of these organs to ensure the lithium carbonate was being flushed through my system.

The word "flushed" is a reminder of a side effect of lithium—thirst. I always have and still drink often and fast; it makes me thirsty. That of course, requires frequent bathroom stops. It's not good when using alcohol though; it's not at all uncommon for me to drink two beers to your one. That's embarrassing, so I try to watch what people around me are

---

[6] Bipolar Disorder, 2014, Francis Mark Mondimore, M.D., Johns Hopkin school of Medicine

drinking and keep the level in my glass the same as theirs. In the end, the frequent drinking of non-alcoholic beverages is effective in cleansing key organs in the body so there isn't a toxic buildup of lithium.

"Unfortunately, Bipolar medications come with some pretty uncommon side effects ... the most common are dry mouth, weight gain, sex drive problems, stomach problems, frequent urination, and appetite changes."[7]

The side effect of weight gain, due to retention of fluids is unfair, in my mind. Add to this the depressive eating habits and my craving for carbohydrates; another side effect of this disorder that can ruin any diet. It's enough to make you depressed all over again. Of course, dieting and exercise diminish both the weight gain and the depression. If I could just find the energy to get off my butt and do it!

The effects of lithium felt like an amputation. I lost the excitement I previously experienced in heightened awareness,

---

[7] Bipolar 101, A Practical Guide;2009 Ruth C. White, PH.D.,MPH,MSW and John D. Preston, PSY.D., ABPP

insight and instantaneous responses to tasks, creativity and problem solving. You might understand this difference in speed if I take your computer away and make you walk to the library to find a book, and then look for information without the speed of technology; a much more time consuming process for the same information. Once you've experienced instant access—you feel it as a traumatic loss.

After a year on lithium, my doctor had me stop taking it for 90 days. The idea was to see if my body had been stimulated to create neuro-chemicals without help. It had not. My behavior was erratic again, so before the 90 days were up I was back on lithium. I've taken lithium every day of my life since then. I mention this fact as important to remember, because all of the incidents I describe occurred while I was taking lithium, as a mood stabilizer, on a daily basis. It scares me to think what might have happened had I taken nothing.

"If you consider the rate of suicide attempts and completion of people with Bipolar disorder and the coincident life disruptions resulting from an episode of mania or depression, then you can consider medications as lifesaving.[8]

---

[8] Bipolar 101 A Practical Guide;2009 Ruth C. White, PH.D.,MPH,MSW and John D. Preston, PSY.D., ABPP

While there are now supplements and complementary therapies available, St. John's Wort and SAM-e have been shown to cause mania when taken by people suffering from Bipolar disorder." (Nierenberg et all. 1999)[9]

For the next thirty-three years my focus was always on the medication. It started with lithium in 1973, after which my doctor added an antidepressant to my treatment plan in 1980. It wasn't until 2007, when my psychiatrist began to open my eyes to other environmental factors, which also have been proven to impact Bipolar disorder. At that time, I began to comprehend the necessity to adjust my own medication as these factors changed.

One might think my story is over at this point. I was diagnosed, and had managed my way to a correct lithium dosage to manage the disease. What more could there be to this chronicle? Well, I've learned Bipolar disorder is never over! It's a part of my everyday life, and it's a road I have had to travel alone, without any involvement from friends or family. You see, when I received my diagnosis in 1973 mental

---

[9] Bipolar 101 A Practical Guide;2009 Ruth C. White, PH.D.,MPH,MSW and John D. Preston, PSY.D., ABPP

illness was hidden and protected from and by families. Disclosure served only to put a cloak of suspicion over everyone in the family.

I have only myself to rely on. Will I always feel the fear? Will I always have to feel I am flying solo through a world of extremes and unpredictability? Will no one else ever see them, feel them, or have the intense need to understand them, as I do?

Expanded vision, accelerated thinking.... that, for me, is the hypomania I experienced before taking lithium. I can best describe it by describing a puzzle test I once took.

With puzzle pieces scattered about, I look at them for only a few seconds before the pattern jumps out at me, showing me how they all go together.

In that test, on that particular day, I completed the puzzle quickly. On the other hand, had I been depressed, it would have taken me five minutes shuffling puzzle pieces, with nothing to show for it but failed attempts and frustration, and no vision at all how the damn puzzle goes together.

INFORMING
MY FAMILY
1973:

———— • ————

SOON AFTER MY discharge from the hospital I had to disclose to my parents just why I had been hospitalized. Obviously, they were extremely curious; over the years, my relationship with them had centered around work and getting into trouble as a teenager.

My wife and I drove to the small town where my parents lived. We were nervous about explaining to them I had a mental disorder. I imagined them being ashamed, annoyed, or angry. I was prepared to deal with any of those emotions. I was, however, totally unprepared for the way they ultimately reacted to my news.

Dad's face remained placid as his eyes rolled into a sideways glance toward my mother. The fire in her eyes matched her stern look, as I spoke. There was a moment of dead silence after I finished, followed by my mother's forceful dismissal of the matter. "That's absurd, there's no mental illness in our family."

My wife and I knew from past experience that this was my mother's standard way of ending conversations she wanted to avoid.

I let out a sign of despair. That was it. Said and done. I wasn't altogether surprised. Since she left her parents' farm, my mother had always wanted everything to be perfect in her life. She wanted material things they never had on the farm, and went to business school so she could make money to buy things she'd always wanted.

My dad comes from a long line of blacksmiths. Apprenticing under my grandfather, he went on to become a Navy welder. When his enlistment was over he worked construction, operated heavy machinery, then built and managed a lime production plant. Dad was a workaholic. I didn't see him much, unless it had something to do with work. We had never functioned as typical father and son.

So, my mother's dismissal wasn't unfamiliar to me, it was just the wrong response at this time and about this issue. My shoulders drooped as I sighed and looked at my wife who only made matters worse when she also rolled her eyes to express her exasperation.

This is it! A cold shoulder. No empathy. No support. Not even recognition that I do have a problem. So, this is how it feels to be so mad you could bite a nail in half!

38

Do they know what they're doing to me?

Age and maturity did not prepare me to deal with my feelings. How could my parents say they love me, but leave

me out to dry when I'm not perfect? I couldn't have felt more abandoned. I left my love for my parents at the door when we left, retaining only an ounce of respect for them.

That respect was good enough to supervise my mother's nursing home care until she passed away. I continue to care for my father, who has dementia. Neither parent ever mentioned my illness after the day I told them. I know now that my mother either had her head in the sand, was grossly wrong, or trying to hide the history of mental illness in our family. Some thirty years after my disclosure I learned about at least two other people on her side of the family who suffered from Bipolar disorder. Both were in the generation following mine. I've also come to suspect one of her brothers had a mood disorder as well. He was always mysteriously absent from family gatherings, blaming farm work needing to be done.

"Several studies show that Bipolar patients often have relatives who also suffer from a Bipolar mood disorder characterized by major depressions and hypomania's… In one study of Bipolar I and II volunteers, 26% of Bipolar II patients had a relative with some kind of psychiatric illness (especially anxiety disorders and addiction), as compared to only 15 % of Bipolar I patients."

POOR JUDGMENT

1973

I am the fool whose life's been spent
Between what is said and what is meant.[10]

———— • ————

THROUGHOUT MY LIFE I've had a sense of adventure. I'd try virtually anything once. After my diagnosis of manic-depression, I began to learn that much of this was associated with a condition termed hypomania. I look at my symptoms of poor impulse control and acting without judgment, and see similar behaviors experienced while growing up.

As a child I would try to find something exciting to do during recess at school. Most of what I did ended in an injury of some kind and landed me in the principal's office. The music room was adjacent to the playground. Believing the music teacher was the one reporting us to the principal, I decided to teach her a lesson. I lit a cherry bomb firecracker

---

[10]©Carrie Newcomer Music, Admin. BMG Chrysalis.

and threw it through her classroom window during her free period. Well, back to the principal's office I went, where the principal explained the room was full of kids making up a class they had missed.

Another time my love of excitement nearly got me killed. Since it was boring to ride our bicycles around the block, we decided it would be more fun to start by the slope of the alley at my house, cross the street, and ride the whole block beyond. As third graders we were smart enough to have a lookout at the street, but that's about all. Of course, it was my turn to race down the alley when the "sentry" was daydreaming or perhaps eating a candy bar. Entering the intersection, I saw a car coming and yelled at our sentry. Braking as hard as I could, my bike slid sideways, slamming my leg and shoulder into the passing car. Looking through the window at the startled man and woman, I shouted, "Sorry, Sir!" He may have said something back to me, but I tore away so fast I never heard it. I've always wondered if his car was damaged.

My early years were also full of mischief, like stealing, smoking, experimenting with sex, and taking my dad's car for joy rides. My actions were impulsive, with total disregard for the rules. I've seen a lot written about if and when children develop Bipolar disorder. One thing I can see now is that I was living between the lines from an early age. Meaning, my inner thoughts created a vision and a plan that defied both common sense and reality. The lack of judgment causing me to act out and carry through a fantasy is something akin to the effects of my Bipolar II disorder. Back then, I was viewed as a naughty boy; perhaps it was nothing more than my brain not working properly.

One thing I have rarely suffered from is indecision. I'm either into something . . . all or nothing. If I'm hypomanic everything seems possible and I don't hesitate. That may be why I experienced a life riddled by difficulties with impulse control and judgment. When feeling depressed, I find myself wallowing in thoughts that cause confusion, and make it impossible to take action.

All my life I've been intrigued by a new adventure. When I was about thirty-years-old I bought a Jeep to challenge the hills and valleys in northeast Iowa. I was proud of my '46 Willy Jeep's capabilities, even if the paint did look pock marked with little red, white and blue chips. I enjoyed driving in one of the Iowa state forests and one day when I had driven an hour to one, I found numerous signs plastered everywhere, stating that it was closed to all 4-wheel drive vehicles.

Oh man! I just drove an hour to get here. That's not fair. Who's going to catch me if I'm only in the forest for a couple of hours?

Ignoring rules, and once again exercising more of my admitted poor judgment, I drove over the cattle guard and went in anyway. Even though it rained a couple of days earlier, I had been cautious enough to wait so everything would be dried out. I knew it wasn't smart to drive on slick trails, so I took all precautions to be safe.

The ground was pretty dry until I turned onto a winding trail on the bank of a ravine. The shaded trail glistened with greasy mud.

It's too late to recover!

I feel the back of the Jeep lighten up and slide toward the ravine. A quick correction and I throw it back on the trail. Down shift, Don, get more control! Now, the Jeep slides in a complete circle; can I catch the edge of the trail? Time seems motionless as I roll down into the ravine.

Luckily I wasn't hurt. The Jeep, leaned on its top, and I felt a flush of emotions crawling out. Feeling stupid, scared, lucky, and afraid of getting caught, and because cell phones were not in existence then, I couldn't call a tow truck or anyone for help. The police scanners would certainly disclose my location, which would mean a state fine for ignoring the warning signs.

All I had was a winch. I don't remember exactly how this "genius" got the Jeep off its top, but I did, using adrenalin, tree branches, and the winch cable. Scared silly, I almost willed that Jeep to move. An hour later I was back on the trail. The tension ran out of me in a rush. Emotionally drained, I wanted someone to beam me up and take me home. I was physically worn out.

I was lucky this time, having come close to real trouble. Extricating myself required quickly learning, without any instructions, to use a winch—all the while under extreme pressure to also solve the bigger problem of making an unobserved escape! If I'd been depressed I would have sat beside the Jeep sorting through all the reasons the trip had gone bad and why I couldn't get myself out of this jam.

I sold the Jeep and bought a Datsun 260Z that I had admired, and became the proud owner and confident driver of a sports car. Soon after I found a two lane road along the Mississippi River's "Great River Road." It was a perfect spot to test drive my sports car. The flat road passed the John Deere factory on the way north, leading to a steep half-mile hill with an "S" curve from bottom to top. I'd start at 70 mph at the bottom, drove wide open through the "S" turns up the hill, and reached 90 mph at the top. A quick downshift and I turned left through a 90-degree corner—the nose of my car sticking to my lane and the back tires sliding across the road—and I would straighten out the car and we sped into a swooping right hand corner. Shifting up in the middle of that corner I'd come out at over 100 mph. You needn't worry, I was cautious enough to stay in my lane. I didn't swerve from lane to lane or threaten anybody's life. After all, I've always been a safe driver!

If this sounds bizarre and dangerous to you, I fully understand; it just didn't seem that way to me. At high speeds like this, I've never been afraid. On the racetrack at Phoenix International Raceway I drove at 145 to 150 mph. Interestingly, everything seemed to move in slow motion. It's exhilarating; it makes me never want to stop. The whole raceway experience was thrilling. When they finally made us stop, I was disappointed, but felt relaxed and calm.

It is important to understand virtually any event or activity performed while I'm hypomanic is an extremely intense one. As a result, when it's over I'm left depleted and exhausted. It's like a 24-hour day crammed into three hours, with all the energy I had available fully consumed.

Fading Love

1974

AFTER MY RELEASE from the hospital in 1973, my wife's behavior changed. No longer a loving, supportive wife, like a mother hen, she treated me as if I were one of the kids. I was no longer a partner in our marriage, but someone who needed close supervision. A leader by nature, I felt forced to follow, always feeling restrained and inadequate.

I've always felt constantly uncomfortable whenever I'm around people who seem healthy and don't have behavioral disorders. I feel self-conscience. They appear consistent and predictable while I am not. So there are always times when I feel inferior to them. What hurts is that I never know when my Bipolar behavior moods are going to happen. Again with the questions . . . always the questions forcing my mind into overtime.

When will my condition be exposed? Will a mood swing affect my behavior. Must I endure their questioning looks while hiding my own shame?

47

Knowing I was always under my wife's watchful eye, I dreaded the moment I might likely do something she deemed wrong. Constant conflict and tension festered between us. I'm sure my mood changes make her insecure. Perhaps the more insecure she became, the more controlling her behavior. She isn't a bad person. But the love between us became as random as two black valentine hearts, somehow lost in a bag of red, heart-shaped candy.

I tried desperately to create a happy family, but could not find compromise within our relationship. I couldn't handle it anymore, which ultimately led to our second separation in 1974, a year after my diagnosis. I didn't go back to the dark and dingy apartment again. Instead, I went to the bluff, and rented an upstairs apartment in an old house.

It made me feel better about myself, but not much else since I was supporting my family as well. That is until I met a woman, just passing through town, who happened to need a place to stay while visiting her dying grandmother. The few weeks she stayed with me and shared the rent made my life much easier. Plus, the companionship helped relieve the depression I had been feeling. She had a motorcycle and we went on weekend rides together. It was exhilarating, just like the days before I started taking lithium. Driving eighty and ninety miles-an-hour on country roads didn't scare me. It may not make sense to most people, but I truly needed this insanity for my sanity.

When the woman left, I took time to revisit my personal situation and fell deep into despair again. A female co-worker noticed me feeling emotionally down and stepped in to help.

We'd been friends for years but I guess she was unhappy at home too, and my need for some warmth in my life brought us together. We developed an intimate relationship that soothed my wounds for a few months.

The relationship ended when she wanted me to leave my children and live with hers. The idea of leaving my boys behind for her children wasn't an option for me, and we went our separate ways. Shortly thereafter, I returned home.

The confusion inside me found its way out while writing down my thoughts. It helped that I could see them and ponder their meaning, like this poem.

Let Me Be Me

Just because I met you today,
Doesn't mean I have to say what you say.
I'm free, so let me be.
I'm a plum and you're acting like a banana

I'm hip, so I'm gonna split.

I'm gonna flee,
before you try to change me.

Just because you don't know
what you want to be,

Can't you just let me be me?

©Don Wooldridge

My behavior during this separation and affair added to problems with my work. With each step up the career ladder came increased interaction with people, more meetings, and more contact with executives. Stress increased even more as I traveled two weeks a month to unknown places across the country to meet people I didn't know. There was pressure to perform regardless whether my Bipolar mood was hypomanic or depressed. This made situations even more unpredictable for me, and increased my fear, since I had no way to prepare for these unexpected and awkward moments.

The personnel manager noticed me on a number of occasions around town and on business trips. I did not leave a good impression on him. He knew I was married and as he watched me go by on a motorcycle with an unfamiliar woman, he wasn't much impressed with me. Neither was he impressed with the stories from fellow employees about my behavior on an Atlanta business trip.

We were at a hotel in Atlanta, Georgia, where my aunt lived. My mother had arranged for us to meet for a brief visit. When she arrived at my hotel with bright red hair, high spiked heels, a short skirt, and a very expensive-looking light blue suede coat, she did not look like anyone's aunt. I had always been embarrassed by her, and only agreed to this meeting at my mother's insistence. When my aunt was walking in a hallway of the hotel none other than the personnel manager asked if he could help her. "Yes," she said, "I'm trying to find Don Wooldridge's room. Do you know where it is?"

An innocent question for her, but a disturbing image for him. I really don't think the explanation I offered later even came close to relieving his concerns.

I can't believe I am doing this to myself! Hiding my illness is exhausting, and now I have to deal with rumors about my behavior with women! No doubt about it... my burden just got heavier.

THE ROAD TO MAYO

1974

———— ♦ ————

AS PART OF our marriage reconciliation my psychiatrist arranged for my wife and me to attend counseling together. We went to a special one-week group therapy at the Mayo Clinic in Rochester, Minnesota. We experienced individual counseling, partner counseling, and group counseling every day for a week. Before we were released, they reviewed their summary analysis with us. It was short-and-sweet: We were incompatible and should not be married.

Even though we understood the message from the professionals, continuing to raise our children as a married couple was important to us. We struggled, and I continued to have plenty of unhappiness, depression, and bouts with suicidal thoughts.

Reflecting on my situation at the time, I knew if we divorced there would be little money left for me. I'd experienced life like that before. If I stayed with my family, at least my children would be close by. I couldn't leave them for at least ten more years. They were so young that I knew if we divorced I would never see them again. I told myself not to leave until their teen years, when they could make their own decisions about their mother and father. Otherwise, my wife would throw up barriers because of my illness and say they wouldn't be safe with me. It was a choice of bearing the pain or losing them forever. I chose the pain.

In the year 2013, a psychologist I've been seeing here in Arizona said it had been a big mistake to put myself in that position after our counseling at the Mayo Clinic. I should not have remained in the marriage. I may have thought it was best for our children, by staying with them another ten years, but it wasn't good for me in light of my mental health and my diagnosed Bipolar II disorder.

"That's too high a price to pay," he said. "It caused you to suffer undue stress, for far too long, exacerbating your Bipolar illness."

I learned from him that each time we separated and left home, I demonstrated my reaction to stress. The only way to get away from the stress and torment was to leave. It became clear stress was the major trigger for the worst of my Bipolar disorder. It seemed to open the door to release all the erratic behavior.

MUTINY

1974

A FEW MONTHS after our return from the Mayo Clinic, the service manager at John Deere expressed interest in transferring me to replace the retiring regional service manager in Toronto, Canada. One helluva promotion! It was exciting for me. I knew the man from our contacts at service meetings around the country; he had taught me a lot about the Canadian region. I loved my experiences working in Canada. Although scared to death about such a big job, I still wanted to try.

The news didn't go over well with my wife. Just like she had done when I graduated from college in Texas, insisting she wouldn't live in Texas, she now refused to live in Canada. I was gravely disappointed. So much so that I considered taking the job and leaving my family behind. I wanted that job, and especially wanted to live in Canada. As one would expect under the circumstances, after turning down the offer, disappointment and anger festered in me, and I found it far too easy to blame my wife for this lost opportunity.

Having refused the promotion, my future in the service organization was over. I was transferred back to the personnel department to oversee all management training. It was not easy—dealing with a deflated ego - but I did my best. I consoled myself that at least I had a job.

CHASING RAINBOWS

1976

AFTER MY TRANSFER from service to personnel, I began to meet and work with many management consultants. I learned quickly what their lifestyle was like. Gradually my interests gravitated to opportunities outside John Deere and a year later, a consultant from Milwaukee, Wisconsin, who was close to Manpower's corporate office notified me of a job opening. Not long afterward I was hired as the director of training and development for Manpower, Inc. to serve their nationwide franchises.

My wife and I needed a fresh start for our marriage. This opportunity offered an escape from the people, places, and things associated with our previous periods of separation. So in 1976 we left Iowa for Milwaukee where I moved my family into a colonial house on one and a half acres.

As I looked back on these jobs many years later, so many things come to light. First of all, I abhor rules and regulations. It was evident just how my wife's constant scrutiny, suspicion, and controlling behavior irritated me . . . add to that the prevailing fear I'd lose my family, the fear my employer would become aware of both my illness, and marital problems—each play a part in driving add to that the prevailing fear I'd lose my family, the fear my employer would become aware of both my illness, and marital problems—each play a part in driving my level of anxiety very high, almost to the point of distraction. That notwithstanding, my depression levels were growing out of control. Sure, lithium controlled the hypomanic moods, but depression had begun to manage my life. Fear, anxiety, stress, and conflict were just about more than I could handle. We tried to save our marriage by moving away; we thought it would work.

I continued using lithium carbonate after we left Iowa. I seemed to do well while we were in Milwaukee. Always a creative person and problem solver, I gained a reputation for successfully developing new systems and departments. In fact, that was my assignment at Manpower: create a training and development department to support the nation-wide franchise system. Our first year in Milwaukee, my boss, the new VP of human resources, expanded the training and employment departments from three to twenty-three people. I developed training programs in customer relations and performance appraisal methods, and traveled throughout the country conducting seminars for Manpower branch managers and employees.

Our marriage settled down in Milwaukee, as I dove into my work and travel, and my wife ran the house without me. I was pleased that our two boys found so much joy in the neighborhood and community. I even coached football and baseball. The edginess of our relationship seemed to have dulled some.

Nothing lasts forever, and in this case, not even a year. At a staff meeting unexpected friction surfaced between the owner/president and the vice president of human resources. "Your objectives are diametrically opposed to my goals," said the president.

Hmmm, better make note of that one.

Clearly seeing the proverbial "writing on the wall," I didn't understand why no one else saw it. Having heard the president's words, it shocked me. He just revealed he was making my boss's sphere of control a target, but as I looked over at my boss, quite frankly I was amazed he didn't really catch on. It was crystal clear to me.

I sought a new job immediately, and was hired by A.O. Smith Corporation just as Manpower laid me off. Again came the questions about how I can hear, understand, and take actions while none of my peers do. In a hypomanic state, I can think and perform well above my normal capabilities. *Can I anticipate future actions?*

I started work at A.O. Smith as the personnel manager for their Data Systems Division. My experiences at John Deere Dubuque Works had included human resources, hiring clerical staff, recruiting engineers, and management training. All of that experience came into play in my new role. A lot of pressure came with it, because the driving force of this division was consistent growth. A case in point: the company replaced its central computer each year I worked there.

I scheduled and participated in 1,000 plus interviews a year. They ranged from college recruiting at Carnegie Melon, Lehigh, Michigan State, and Purdue, etc. as well as employment agencies. In addition to the repetition of recruiting interviews, I had to manage the daily salary and benefits administration for current employees.

Having an insensitive, "bottom line" boss didn't fit me well. Again, being averse to rules, regulations, processes, and procedures, I struggled, even as I excelled at recruiting. Although everyone involved thought I was doing a good job, the wear and tear on my emotions was continuous.

I have come to realize left brain thinkers, like my boss, manage bottom line facts without emotion. They are completely opposite my right-brained creative thinking and problem solving. Therein lies the pressure, friction, and stress that are deadly to my emotional behavior and moods. I hung in there primarily because my family liked Milwaukee so much.

Late in 1979, a recruiter flattered me by offering me a job in Battle Creek, Michigan. Clark Equipment's Lift truck division wanted me to build a service training department like I'd done for John Deere. I had loved my position with John Deere. *Could I repeat my success at Clark Equipment? Would I be as happy?* Full of hope, we moved to Michigan.

What I didn't know beforehand, as I tried to seek a new work environment that would allow my wife and me to have a reasonably successful marriage, I was actually headed toward the same environment that I had tried to escape in Iowa.

SECTION II

MY REARVIEW MIRROR

FILTERS

1980

———— ◆ ————

We move forward one-step at a time,
Wide-eyed and hopeful, lost and half-blind.
Mistake by mistake, we all learn to be kind.
There is so much to see and to realize,
If I could close my mouth and open my eyes[11]

KALAMAZOO, MICHIGAN, IS where we settled, only thirty minutes from my job in Battle Creek. Wonderful community . . . wonderful neighborhood . . . redo of a rotten marital relationship.

Starting a new job is always stressful, and I had eight new positions over the ten years I worked at John Deere. Add my move to Manpower and A.O. Smith in Milwaukee, and now

---

[11] ©Carrie Newcomer Music, Admin. BMG Chrysalis.

Clark Equipment and you have a total of eleven new responsibilities in thirteen years. The drive to be accepted and successful created a lot of stress and fatigue for me; it was aggravated by trying to keep my Bipolar illness a secret. My behavior started to reflect this tension. Unfortunately, I had yet to understand how integrally stress did affect my overall behavior. Although I continued my medication, my moods seemed mostly depressed.

My new job at Clark Equipment and the required travel forced my wife to continue running the household by herself. Our children were twelve and nine years old, and my absence allowed a method of parenting to evolve that excluded me when I was at home. I think every man has an agenda of things he thinks boys should know—learning to manage money, being responsible, developing good work habits, and so on.

Unfortunately, yet not totally unexpected, my strong emotional upheavals recurred in Michigan. It was obvious to us I needed help, so in 1980 I found a local psychiatrist: Dr. Dunstone.

At my first appointment he commented, "Don, I see you were diagnosed back in 1973 as manic-depressive."

"Yes, that's right."

"Well, Don, manic-depressive illness research had come a long way since your diagnosis. What I see here in your chart and hear as you describe your behavior indicates to me that your illness is not manic-depression, but a condition we have recognized and now call Bipolar. Your euphoric episodes certainly don't appear to be as extreme or destructive as manic episodes.

The doctor put down his chart and looked up at me. "We call these lesser episodes "hypomanic."

"So I'm not as bad as they thought?"

"Well, that's not entirely true," he said. "Your depressive episodes can be just as extreme as manic-depression. Under the current circumstances, I feel we need to focus your treatment on your depression. I want to start you on an anti-depressant medication, and we'll monitor your behavior weekly as we search for the proper dosage."

In spite of my concern, the anti-depressant medication worked for me. Interestingly enough, anti-depressants and Bipolar disorder are not known to mix, as reported by Dr. Francis Mark Mondimore.

"The depression of Bipolar disorder is much more difficult to treat than manic or mixed states... individuals have more problem with depression than with mania and these depressions can be especially long, debilitating, and difficult to treat.

The role of anti-depressants in the treatment of Bipolar disorder—whether persons with Bipolar disorder should even take anti-depressants—remains a matter of debate among experts…this is because these medications can push a Bipolar patient from depression into a manic state." [12]

In the process of getting my dosage right, another phenomenon happened that shook me to the bone. My wife and I attended a costume party in our neighborhood. I thought it was hilarious and a lot of fun. My best friend dressed in pink tights and leotards that fit his 6 ft. 2 in. and 200-pound frame. I had a great time and was feeling good as we got in the car to go home. But, as we drove away my wife lit into me. She scolded me fiercely about my behavior. She railed on and on about how I had been loud, rude, and obnoxious. I had totally embarrassed her, and if I ever did it again, she'd never go anywhere with me. Wow! So much for my good spirits.

After my wife's tirade, I immediately withdrew into my thoughts and sorted through the events of the night. I saw nothing in my memory of the party that should have upset her. I hoped that we could just forget it, but when it happened two

---

[12] Bipolar Disorder, 2014, Francis Mark Mondimore, M.D., Johns Hopkins School of Medicine

or three more times during that year I became seriously confused.

The overriding fear within me escalated. My self-confidence shredded, I became uncomfortable knowing I couldn't even trust myself. If I couldn't tell the difference between my perception and reality, how could I tell if I was doing something wrong? When would I be offensive, obnoxious, unacceptable, or embarrassing again? I felt like a social pariah.

How in the world can I hide my illness from friends and co-workers if I don't even know what I am doing? My illness could be exposed and I wouldn't even know it!

As far as I was concerned, my Bipolar life was like living with a mischievous shadow that followed me around causing trouble, like this:

Let's say I'm walking down the sidewalk and pass by a restaurant's outdoor patio. An attractive women is exiting, so I stop to let her by. She says, "Thank you," and I say "Your welcome, ma'am." But my naughty, Bipolar shadow pinches her on the butt, causing her to whirl and slap me in the face. Looking like a jerk, I'm left taking responsibility for bad behavior that I really had nothing to do with.

Beginning with the night of the party, and for the rest of my life, I've lived with the fear that I'll be responsible for something I'm not aware of. Not the kind of fear you'd feel if you were hanging by your feet over an open well. Or the kind of fear you'd feel in a war zone crawling on the ground with bullets flying over your head. I'm talking about the fear you'd feel when someone is stalking you, yet wherever you look you can't see the stalker. You'd be cautious of every move and look for your stalker before each step. And that's how I feel every waking moment of my life. Let me give you another example:

Assume you met with your child's principle to discuss a conflict between your pediatrician's orders regarding your child's outdoor activities, and the teacher's choice to ignore the restrictions. You feel good about yourself. You thought you made your point, and the school would adjust their response to honor your child's needs.

The next day your child tells you the principal and teacher were very upset about your tone and verbal dressing down of the principal and the school. Now your child remains in the classroom during recess, and punished with extra work that must be done by the time the class returns.

"What!" You say, "That's outrageous! I did not do that."

But understand that this is the type of feedback I can get, anytime. It has happened often. That's why I am so conscience where I am, who I am with, and the number of people with whom I surround myself. Then, I'm still anxious until tomorrow when I can see or hear reactions to my "yesterday."

To live with this constant fear, I had to develop a defense mechanism. To manage the anxiety I have in social situations, I've needed to have a sort of out-of-body experience. I try to observe myself, the situation I'm in, and how people react to me in the moment. Because I'm disconnected from my actual behavior, in every interpersonal encounter every day of my life, it's not uncommon for me to watch for clues from others about my behavior. Like the rolling eyes of a lizard in search of prey, I watch your eyes:

> To read your reaction to my emotions.
> To judge my social impact.
> To see if I'm behaving acceptably.
> To see if your joy allows me to relax.
> To look for anxiety causing me to withdraw into myself.

With practice, I find that I can observe the effect I'm having in a one-on-one situation. I'm even good enough to judge the feedback of my behavior with two other people. But not three. With three people, there's always one person that I can't observe, or be able to judge their attitudes or reactions to me. That being the case, I know there's a high risk that I will say or do something that's offensive to some person in the group. Discussing this with my doctor I was surprised to learn that Bipolar disorder comes with filters.

Really? Filters? Really? That's all I need. Another reason to monitor my behavior!

One reason I don't know my behavior is bad is because some filter prevents me from noticing the intensity of my actions. My mind sees things the way I intend them to be, but the outside world sees what I'm doing as it actually occurs.

I'm very disturbed by this information.

With my doctor's help, I learned my Bipolar disorder filters out anger and sarcasm. I can only gauge how my emotions are received by observing the reaction of people around me. I've also learned that I can easily be viewed as disruptive, just because I don't understand the timing of my statements, or the impact they will have on others. Because my brain processes abstract information slowly, the timing of my statements can appear out of place and disruptive. My personality doesn't help either because I'm a ruminative thinker, meaning I think through a problem over and over and over. Just like a cow's digestive system. I also view a problem from all sides, like spokes on a wagon wheel. And then I tend to speak in summaries, like the following example:

During a product review meeting at Creative Universal Training Consultants, the topic concerned the sequence of events necessary to roll out the service advisor's seminars. I sensed something wasn't right and my mind stayed glued to the sequence of events. As the conversations continued, I chose to analyze the sequence, picturing the dealership shop, the customer's entry, and the activities that followed. I walked myself through the whole process and found that it was actually out of order, compared to actual practices in Ford dealerships.

"Excuse me, but this sequence is wrong," I said, interrupting the group.

"I'm sorry," the moderator said. "Why didn't you say so earlier?"

"Because I didn't know then," I said.

"Well, how do you know it's wrong now? What evidence do you have?"

"I know it's wrong because I've been in a dealership. I know it's wrong because I've walked through the process. It involves two other departments and just can't work this way without their participation," I said.

"I hate to say this," the moderator said. "But until you can provide documentation that this sequence is wrong, we're going to move on."

It infuriates me when I have the answer, yet have to travel through the maze of uninformed doubters to prove it. It seems to me that those who are not problem solvers require a detailed script to follow through life, while problem solvers evaluate cause and effect, weigh the alternatives, make a decision, and then move on.

RAGE

1980

————— ✦ —————

I shook my fist,
I left too soon,

The soft wounded animal inside of me,
Stood up on its hind legs and howled at the moon.
Anger rises,
In a violent storm,
And when I am the wisest
I lay down beside it,
And hum in its ear, until it gets quiet.[13]

DEALING WITH MARITAL problems was part of my psychotherapy in 1980. At one point, Dr. Dunstone invited my wife to come with me. She was extremely reluctant, and had to be reminded of our appointment and coaxed to attend.

Around the third or fourth visit together, when he began to discuss her behavioral issues, she left the room and never

---

[13] ©Carrie Newcomer Music, Admin. BMG Chrysalis.

returned. Around the third or fourth visit together, when he began to discuss her behavioral issues, she left the room and never returned.

My doctor asked me, "How do you feel about her leaving, Don?"

"I'm furious. After all I've been through. All the doctors and medications I'd dealt with over the years. The fear of my behavior and exposure of my illness I've experienced each and every minute of every day. It's all too easy to tell she doesn't care."

"Now, Don, she didn't say that."

"She didn't have to. After the commitment I've made to get well and be a good husband, she turned her back when she could do something to help us. That told me right then and there she'll never be a partner in my battle with Bipolar disorder. I'm in this alone. Forever!"

"I'm really very sorry this happened to you, Don," Dr. Dunstone said.

He suggested my wife have individual treatment as well, but it never happened. Without correcting her behaviors, we had no chance of making the marriage work.

It is clear that she wants all of the problems with our relationship to be mine. No cooperative effort.

Nothing good was going to happen until I got myself fixed… something that can't happen with any permanent mental disorder.

All she leaves me with is feeling beyond alone, with the weight of the world on my shoulders.
Where do I go? What do I do?

I continued to feel like an outsider at home, struggling for equality in our parenting roles. I have a vivid memory of our oldest son arriving home way past his curfew.

"Son, do you have an explanation for why you're home an hour late?" I asked.

"I had car trouble, Dad, and thought I could fix it in time."

"And you never thought of calling us to let us know what happened, and why you'd be late?"

"I didn't think it would be necessary, Dad."

"Well, it is necessary for us to know what's happening to you when you're away. And to help you remember, I'll need your car keys. You'll get them back in a week."

"Don't you dare," my wife said. "That won't be necessary." Stepping between my son and me she snarled, "I'll handle this."

Looking at our son she said, "You know the rules. You're grounded for two weeks, and that's that."

Grabbing her shoulders I pulled her around to face me, and asked, "Why the hell would you ground him for two weeks? The problem is him and his car. That's why I don't want him to drive."

"I know what's best for him," she said. "You're not around here enough to know."

I was furious. We engaged in a vicious argument. When it ended, she turned to where our son had been standing. He was gone. We found him asleep in his bed.

Events like this can put me into a rage, and I experienced them far too often during this time in our marriage.

Rage is hard for a companion or care giver to understand. How does rage differ from just plain old anger? It looks the same, doesn't it? Perhaps it does on the outside, but certainly not from the inside. Personally, it feels more like a barometer inside my chest, with only a few levels of readings; like "Cool," 'Happy," "Irritated," "Angry," and "Rage." I can feel it inside when the pressure builds and the rage tries to get out. I can feel it boil like a volcano, heating up, vibrating my body, and blinding my reason. When it explodes, I can't control it. I'd warn my wife, "Don't say another word. Leave me alone!" I need a quiet place to cool off."

Sadly, she is a person who needs the last word, so instead of honoring my request, she ignored my warning, and continued her tirade against me.

BOOM! I explode; without reason, I leap out of the brush like a wild gorilla and attack the irritating noise. The one who wouldn't shut up like I had warned them. Yelling, screaming, and blindly swinging... almost unconsciously I would do just about anything to stop that irritating noise. SHUT UP! SHUT UP! SHUT UP!

My rage is very dangerous to all concerned. And when I come to my senses and return to reality, I'm left with deep feelings of remorse, shame, and guilt. Immediately, I want to do anything possible to make things the way they were before I damaged them.

I've heard of mixed episodes related to manic-depression, but could never explain it. I was soon to learn, however, mixed states of mind in Bipolar patients are considered very dangerous.

Dr. Mondimore's book, *Bipolar Disorder*, explained a mixed state of mind in this way:

"This mood, a strange combination of both the frenzied intensity of mania and the horrors of deep depression, has been called a mixed state."[14]

---

[14] Bipolar Disorder, 2014, Francis Mark Mondimore, M.D., Johns Hopkins School of Medicine

Dr. Kay Jamison, a psychiatrist at Johns Hopkins University School of Medicine made the following comment about mixed states.

"On occasion, these periods of total despair would be made even worse by terrible agitation."[15]

---

15 Bipolar An Unquiet Mind, Kay Redfield Jamison, PhD, Johns Hopkins School of Medicine

SUICIDE

1980

OVER TIME, MY wife's constant criticism destroyed my self-esteem. It was crushed. The whole situation caused me to become severely depressed, then suicidal, only because I could see no other way out. Of course, I could leave and relieve the pain, but my depression left me paralyzed and immobile. My mind dwelt on suicide but my body didn't want to move. I can't tell you how many nights at two or three a.m. I sat on the living room couch staring out the window watching the snowflakes fall around the yard light—thinking suicide, suicide, suicide—every night. It would be the easy way out. I wouldn't have to deal with the pain of my decision. I wouldn't have to explain myself to anybody. My wife and kids would be free of conflict. Suicide… suicide… suicide.

But I'm not mad at my two boys. My wife is the one that drives me to distraction. What if I killed her? I could shoot her. Maybe suffocate her in bed tonight. Or, I could drown her.

That's kind of stupid. I'd be in jail and the boys in foster care.
Would I be okay in jail? It could be a safe place for me.
I wouldn't have to hide my illness anymore. But it wouldn't be
fair to my boys. Their life would be miserable because of me.

According to Kay Jamison of the Johns Hopkins University School of Medicine (2000), "At least 25 to 50 percent of people with Bipolar disorder attempt suicide at least once, and mood disorders are the most common psychiatric conditions associated with suicide."[16]

Though I was severely depressed, I had to continue working or my mental health issue would be discovered. But it was almost more than I could manage; I'd collapse when I returned home. Combine the depression and working long hours with my overall lack of sleep, I was continually exhausted. How I functioned I don't know, but the nights I stared out the window at the light I felt almost zombie-like... much the same as I had looking out the window of the hospital watching a squirrel play on the tree.

---

16   Bipolar An Unquiet Mind, Kay Redfield Jamison, PhD, Johns Hopkins School of Medicine

THRILL RIDE

1981

———— • ————

IN ADDITION TO working with TV writers, producers, and directors, I had some other interesting experiences working for Clark Equipment. Because of my success developing and presenting training programs, other divisions of Clark requested my services. One of the first was our overseas division.

I had successfully presented a two-day technical trainer certification program for U.S. service managers, with a two-day follow up "certification" class that verified participants could actually use the skills. The German factory wanted this two-part course delivered over the course of five straight days.

In Germany, the Muhlheim factory's service department supported all of Western Europe's Clark dealerships. France and Germany had the most dealers, of course, and were the closest to the Muhlheim, Germany factory.

The factory's service department asked me to schedule three weeks in June to work with them. The first week they sent me to visit a dealership in Stockholm, Sweden. The second week I taught a seminar in Basingstoke, England, and another seminar in Muhlheim, Germany the third week.

What an experience! I don't want to take forever recounting all that happened, but it was a blast. Challenging yes, but what a fun adventure! Take, for instance, my class in England. Besides the English, this group included participants whose native languages were French, German, Flemish, Swedish, and Danish. No one had warned me. That's the group I was expected to teach, and there was no way out of it.

I found the challenge stimulating, and exciting. In minutes I created a solution on my feet. I found the most skilled English speaker in each language group and made him their leader. After teaching a skill, I'd give each group leader time to teach his comrades. What a cacophony of sounds! They would ask their questions via their leader, and then I'd proceed with new information. They gave me all the attention and respect I'd ever enjoyed, until the Pub opened... at which time I suddenly faced an empty room.

My trip from England to Germany was also quite the adventure. Two participants from Western Europe had each rented a car in Dover, England, but needed to get back to work quickly and flew home from London. That meant the service training manager and I had to return the cars to Dover, where we'd then catch a Hovercraft to Calais, France.

I had to resolve problems on the fly, which excited me and heightened my mental capabilities. First there was driving on the left side of the road to conquer. Second was driving a "round about" in the opposite direction from what I was used to. And lastly, I lost my leader for a few moments in the English city of Dover. I loved it! Challenging. Exciting. Rewarding. Each spells adventure for me.

The Dover Hovercraft port and staging area was utterly confusing to me. It looked like a boat dock, but everything I saw reflected an airport terminal. There were flight check in signs, flight departure signs, and ticket counters just like American air carriers. Did they expect the Hovercraft to drop in out of the air?

We were outside the terminal leaning on a fence when the Hovercraft finally came in. Unbelievably, it left the water of the English Channel about one-half mile away, and glided up the sandy beach to the terminal like a kid would play with a toy. Huge rubber bumpers all around, with two helicopter blades turning on top. What a thrilling sight.

The jaws of this creature opened and loaded lines and lines of cars, and trucks. Then people filled the upper decks. The trip across the English Channel to Calais, France was exciting. We wove our way across the channel traffic of freighters and cruise ships.

I'm feeling it! It's Exciting!
The adventure, creativity, and stimulation
of new and different environments is quite.
different from the moods I experience at home.

In the fall I was surprised to learn that Clark Equipment had a division named Horizon Credit that financed yachts. They asked me to train their staff in the Xerox Sales and Customer Service techniques. So I went to Ft. Lauderdale, Florida for a couple weeks.

I would teach one group for half of the week while the others kept the office running, and then swapped staff and teach the other group for the second half of the week. A few months later I taught the second course in the same manner. Very nice people, and very interesting business. I was fascinated... at the time they financed no watercraft worth less than $500,000. Those were new numbers for me, for sure, but it was the accommodations that were most impressive. I was accustomed to staying in motels for years, and the B&B's of Germany; on this trip I stayed on a yacht. Surprise! Why would Horizon Finance put me in a hotel when they have three or four repossessed yachts sitting in the marina? Taking me to the marina, they asked, "Which yacht would you like to stay on this week?"

Picture me sitting on this big chair in back of the boat, sipping a beer as I watched the sunset. There was always someone to talk to as people moved up and down the dock. I felt special and my thoughts were positive.

The participants in my classes are enthusiastic. I'm on top of the world. My mood is skyrocketing.

EUPHORIA

1982

———— • ————

WORKING FOR CLARK Equipment I wrote and produced technical training programs on video tape. I found two things: it was very interesting, but like many things for me, could become routine. When new technology allowed self-paced learning systems on video tape I began writing and producing interactive training programs. My excitement was renewed by this new technology. With the help of equipment from Panasonic U.S. and training by Sony Video Utilization Services in Hollywood, California, I was certified as an Interactive Learning System Programmer. That meant that I could design and program linear and dynamic branching self-paced learning systems on videotape or videodisc. Those systems were cutting edge in the market place at the time.

Diving right in, I began to design and produce courses on this new medium. My favorite was the dynamic branching technique.

Wow! Was I made for this or what?

Dynamic branching design is addictive for me. It takes the learner, who answered a learning module incorrectly, back into the learning segment for remedial training. In this way, each learner gets a personalized training session. That's easy to say, but the actual difficulty of the designing process is what turned me on.

To simplify the process for you, picture a checker board and all its squares. In the design process some squares move the lesson forward, and others take it backward to remedial lessons. It was my job to decide which square did what, and then connect them so the media program played them in the correct progression. In our video studio each square would be a scene, then edited in the sequence that I designed.

My mood had elevated, allowing me to easily lay out this checkered schematic in my head and visualize just how the media would play. It was thrilling and was the perfect place for me.

What a terrific respite from my turmoil and depression. I put my marriage problems behind me and focused completely on this highly creative process. I love it. I might even get some recognition out of it!

Dr. Tom Dargan, a consultant for the Sony Video Utilization Services, had been my instructor. He also collaborated with me in developing a self-paced learning system. Our Clark Production Studio produced the video program using stunt drivers from Hollywood who rolled lift trucks off ramps and loading docks.

The Director of Educational Research at Western Michigan University helped me create the research process and statistical analysis of the results.

We named the project "The Great Betrayal." Its purpose was to utilize self-paced learning so lift truck drivers could practice their decision-making during a lift truck rollover. The key was to forewarn them 'not to jump' if their vehicle rolled over. Staying inside the lift truck is the only way to prevent quadriplegic injury.

When the project was completed in August of 1983, International Television Magazine asked Dr. Dargan and me to write an article titled, "Linear vs. interactive videotape training." I was flying high, thinking I had finally found my calling. When I'm hypomanic anything is possible, and I was ready to make things happen.

ENTREPRENEUR
1983

———— • ————

"**THE GREAT BETRAYAL**" was so successful I wanted to produce more. Unfortunately, Clark Equipment didn't share my enthusiasm. Plans to provide equipment to dealerships so they could play back self-paced video programs were shelved. No new projects were planned and I was forced to return to developing traditional video training programs… my thoughts were rather explosive.

This isn't good enough for me! I'm on a high. I have special skills. Creativity is like a drug, and I want more of it. I have to have it!

To satisfy a serious unmet need, I created a sole proprietorship called Interactive Learning Systems and promoted my service to other businesses that had highly technical Zero Tolerance processes and procedures. My time after work at Clark was spent doing a lot of "show and tell" to satisfy curiosity. I sold only small demos for the curious. By this time my hypomania had waned, and I was starting to get depressed. The glow was gone. Reality was setting in... and self-doubt grew like a cancer.

Only six months into my new venture, my boss told me the human resources department had ordered him to inform me that Clark considered my outside activities a conflict of interest. My ears perked up when I heard that. Initially, Clark had involved me in this activity but now was not interested in using it beyond our recent research. Now, all of a sudden I'm being singled out? Because I had no income from my venture to sustain me, I had to cease and desist. I swallowed my pride, and lost all the money I'd invested in time and equipment.

A few weeks later, Clark Equipment found themselves in financial trouble. There was talk of layoffs, similar to my experience at Manpower in Milwaukee, but my boss assured me I didn't need to worry; I did anyway.

Watching closely I saw people laid off here and there. Finally I was left with just two of my previous 15 employees. Then, besides hourly employees, 500 salaried employees were also laid off. Everyone panicked and started looking over their shoulders. A huge meeting was held, including both hourly and salaried employees. Management's message was that layoffs were complete and we were the key people who remained to keep the operation viable.

"Don't worry," the general manager said, "You can buy those new homes, new cars, and lawn mowers now. Layoffs are over, and you can relax." Unfortunately, many employees did what he said.

But, it smelled like a rat to me, and I started looking for a job right away. Here again, it seemed I was the only one who realized the need to take action to keep ahead of the impending trouble. My mind saw it clearly; a reflection of what I did with Manpower, when I had found a new job just before being laid off.

DIVORCE

1984

———◆ ◆———

EXPERIENCING THE THRILLS, excitement, and happiness that were the reward of my interactive video projects, the indecision concerning my marriage started to fade away. I still held out hope, but on my second trip to Germany, in 1984, the regional training manager encouraged me to bring my wife, at the company's expense. She being of German decent, I thought taking her would be perfect; it was anything but.

She expected everything to be about her, and with everything done just the way she expected things to be. But, this trip was special and I wanted it to be a memorable one. So, every time she criticized me, I tried to change to become more acceptable. I changed, and I changed, and I changed. I ended up just going in circles, screwing myself into the ground like an auger. The criticizing, condemning, and complaining went on until I literally had no self-esteem left.

I think at times we are reminded of the exact moment our life changed. This is certainly true in the course of my marriage. It is clear the tipping point came while standing on the steps of the Cathedral of Koln, Germany in a very loud and heated argument with far too many people on the plaza watching and listening. Remembering, I can honestly say I have never felt more ridiculous and embarrassed in my life. I had expected her to be grateful; instead, she remained hateful. It was then I made my decision. When we returned home I filed for divorce.

Our divorce became a continuation of our marriage, of course. Fighting, kicking, and screaming all the way. I just wanted to get it over with, and she wanted to punish me until I bled to death. I filed in 1984, not anticipating it would go on for two long years.

My loss of friends was immediate: the women who sided with my wife would not allow their husbands to communicate with me. As I watched their actions and listened to the words of our friends and neighbors, I got a sense of their point of view, of which I wrote as in the following poem.

Deceased

Their divorce is like a death,
It takes away your breath.

It's something we didn't conceive,
And simply can't believe.

We've known them all our lives,
And they acted like most husbands and wives.

The thing that haunts me,
Is the trouble and strife we didn't see.

We feel it could have been greed,
But I guess they each have a separate need.

And, while we helplessly ponder why,
We watch another marriage die.

©Don Wooldridge

TRANQUILITY
1984

WITH THE DIVORCE process underway, positive things began to happen for me, including a two-bedroom apartment into which I moved. This time I knew living alone would be permanent, though my furnishings were not. In the living room a packing box held up my TV, and I watched it sitting on the bottom half of a trundle bed. The other half was in my bedroom. A card table and chairs were in the kitchenette, and all of my plastic utensils came from our camping gear. Although I considered my furnishings disappointing, I wasn't depressed. After all, I had escaped the stress and turmoil of our marriage. I was feeling fine and optimistic.

Living alone was very good for me and allowed me to focus and create my own personal routines. I reserved Saturday's for laundry and cleaning and Sunday's for cooking, so all my meals were ready for the week. Of course, I kept frozen dinners on hand for the lazy days. Saturday nights I went out to eat, and my ironing got done watching Monday Night Football.

I can imagine most people would think this a normal, simple, and redundant life. Maybe so, but it was a big deal to me. It's the first time in my life I had a routine and the happiest with myself I'd ever experienced. I'd never been able to find the discipline to formulate new routines. I miss that developmental part of my life, and sometimes feel like a lesser person for not continuing a stringent routine in my life.

One of the keys to managing Bipolar disorder is routine; it's suggested in many books on the subject. Bipolar patients are encouraged to be in bed at the same time every day to produce the consistent sleep patterns we need to stabilize our moods. It's also recommended that we wake up at the same time of day. Eating habits, drinking habits, and exercise habits all fit into this concept of routine. Unknowingly, what I experienced during the time I lived in the apartment helped moderate and manage my Bipolar disorder during a highly stressful divorce process.

Once settled in my new apartment, I tried to renew my career as well. Inspired by the research work I experienced at Clark Equipment, I wanted to pursue a Master's Degree in Industrial Psychology. I subsequently passed the Graduate Record Examination, which qualified me to enter graduate school, and I began taking courses at Western Michigan University. About mid-semester I felt it important to arrange a meeting with the Psychology department head to inquire about employment options. It was really upsetting. There I was, only forty-three years old, and he referred to me as "old."

He went on to say, "Mr. Wooldridge, a master's degree would be a waste of your time. By the time you complete your degree you'll be too old to find a job, either in the marketplace or a university staff."

I was crushed, and sure as hell didn't intend to spend time in his department if he had that attitude. Dr. Dargan mentioned that the University of Nebraska offered a degree in the design and programming of self-paced learning systems, and that was an option, as well. I guess I just wasn't ready to leave my children forever, so I never applied to Nebraska.

This was a serious personal disappointment, and caused me to feel tied down. For many months after I drowned my sorrows at the local pubs, developing a set of acquaintances that I'd meet on Saturday nights. Over time it became a bore; I had to get a life.

COMPANIONSHIP

1985

———— • ————

AFTER MANY MONTHS of just hanging out, I tired of the sameness and left the bar scene and made myself a promise to go my own way, but not spend my time pursuing opportunities to meet women. If there was going to be another woman in my life, she would just have to show up where I was, doing the same things. A very comfortable and uncomplicated strategy! Being away from constant marital conflict, I felt great and was able to avoid excessive hypomania and depression.

I returned to our local church, having stayed away during the divorce process and foreclosure because my wife and the boys continued to attend there. I didn't want the contact. But after our house foreclosed and they moved, they joined another church in town.

One day while singing bass in the back row of the choir, I noticed a woman two rows ahead of me in the soprano section. Her name was Pat. On this occasion I saw her in a new light.

We both had interest in Big Ten sports, and she would needle me about Iowa and I returned the favor regarding Michigan State. It had been lighthearted for years, like "Good morning, Pat, your green team was so slow yesterday they looked like part of the turf," kind of humor.

I had heard that she was a widow; her husband had died years ago. When a choir rehearsal ended early one evening, I wondered how I could get to know her better. I took a chance and asked her to stop for a glass of wine at a small restaurant on our way home. She accepted, and during our conversation I learned then that she had actually been divorced for nine years, from the former basketball coach and athletic director at the local high school. She wasn't lonely or despondent at all. In fact, she had a strong sense of independence.

I'm sure it wasn't love at first sight because she quickly downed the last of her wine, stood up and said, "I have got to go. My dog hasn't been out to pee since noon. Thanks so much for inviting me. Sorry."

I get to sit alone while some dog that has to pee gets her attention?

In the end, I must have made some kind of impression because she accepted my invitation to attend a 4th of July party at a lake, put on by a fellow employee. After eating, someone yelled, "Anybody want to water ski?"

"Sure," I said, as I looked around for Pat and found her in the boat. Well, this was going to be fun. I used to be a kick-ass water skier growing up. A neighbor girl and I even talked about going to Florida together and trying out for the Cypress Gardens ski show. I was ready to show my stuff.

Watch this!

We were all in the boat and the driver said, "Who's first?" "I'll go first," I said, "Where are the skis?"

Too late. I saw Pat already in the water with the skis, holding tight to the ski rope.

What's with this woman anyway!

We had a great day, in spite of some surprises. When we were leaving, Pat asked me to stop by her house for supper. I got directions, and we both started out together. Moving through town about 5 mph over the speed limit, I expected to be waiting in her driveway when she arrived. Not true. Her car sat in the driveway when I arrived.

Damn! People don't beat me like this. I'm usually first.

Pat didn't need a man in her life, and in the process of getting a divorce, I didn't need a permanent relationship in my life either. As a result, our relationship developed slowly and at arm's length. I enjoyed having a female companion now and then. She was very thoughtful. Because I didn't have much money, Pat would make dinner at home before we'd go out dancing. Being in her home was comfortable, and a brief escape from my apartment.

Many months later when Path's birthday came, we were still dating. Fortunately, I had learned enough about her to write a poem for her birthday gift. I was pleased with myself that I could write something positive without being in either a depressed or a hypomanic mood.

To the Ladies I Love

Happy Birthday they all will say,
Wishing their friend Pat a happy day.

So on this your special day,
Permit me to say it another way.

Happy birthday to practical Pat,
Who refuses to play,
'Til household matters are out of the way.

Happy Birthday to the physical Pat,
For when you're working around your home,
There isn't a thing you can't do alone.

Happy Birthday to Pat, the mother,
Whether a listening ear or an onward cheer,
You make it known that you are near.

Happy Birthday to Grandma Pat,
She will appear at the drop of a hat,
It just depends where Lauren's at.

Happy Birthday to Pat, my friend,
No matter if I'm up or down,
Your warmth is always around.

Happy Birthday to the gracious lady,
To young and old who pass her way,
All are blessed with a brighter day.

Happy Birthday to the lady on my arm,
With her magnetism,
and attractive charm.

Happy birthday my precious one,
Without you here life just can't be fun.
I celebrate this special day with all of you.

©Don Wooldridge

Was I Manic?

1985

———— ◆ ————

A FEW WEEKS later an associate in Detroit called me about a service training project with a consulting firm in Warren, Michigan. I pursued the opportunity, landing the job with Creative Universal. Pat stayed in Kalamazoo while I moved to an apartment in Madison Heights, Michigan. We saw each other on weekends when we could.

I was hired by Creative Universal as a division manager, reporting to the president, Mr. Short. He was a wonderful, honest, and trustworthy man, but a master manipulator.

I learned about the manipulation part during my job interview. My initial interview with numerous people on the staff apparently went well because he invited me back for an interview with his partner, dinner, and a weekend stay in an upscale hotel in Birmingham, Michigan.

After a very nice dinner at an exclusive restaurant, Mr. Short said, "I think I'll have an after-dinner drink, how about you?"

"Well, okay," I said Maybe this was his way of kicking back and just talking. I wasn't sure.

"Do you like Rusty Nails?" he asked. "They're my favorite. You ought to try one."

We chatted while sipping our drinks. "Let's have another one. Waiter!" he said.

Hmm, I'd better be careful. These are strong drinks.

Careful for sure, because we had four Rusty Nails after dinner. Not quick enough to figure it out at the time, he had been testing me to see if I could hold my liquor when entertaining clients that drank a lot.

Thank God, I didn't pass out or fall face first onto the table. When he was ready to leave, I simply got up, walked to the car, and drove to the motel. Guess I passed, because I got the job.

Man, this job is a breath of fresh air. Rebirth! Now's my chance to recover financially and emotionally.

My first day on the job, Mr. Short sent me out to dinner with one of his longtime clients and friends. After dinner we talked business at my hotel for an hour or two before we split up for the night. The next day, the president called me into his office first thing. "Just what did you say or do last night?" he asked. "Our client was really upset, and called me last night saying that you were bullying him, and then he told me he wouldn't work with you and that he wouldn't recommend that I hire you."

Oh man, what happened? I never saw it that way, and thought we were getting along quite well. Am I stupid? Totally inept? Or did my Bipolar problem happen at just the wrong time?

Whatever it was... fatigue, alcohol, stress, or a Bipolar incident, I almost lost this job.

"If I ever hear of this happening again, it will be the last time you represent this company!" Mr. Short said.

Wow, what a great start, eh?

After years of retrospection I'm sure my Bipolar disorder contributed in some way. It must have, causing me to be blind to what I said and did. In good conscience who would do something so stupid? I feel the cruelty of disappointment, guilt and anguish when I see the effects of what I've done, and don't have the privilege to press "delete" to correct or remove the offending behavior. Understandably, my level of fear shot up dramatically. Like a fawn hiding in the grassy mound of an open field, I constantly monitored the reactions of people who might feel the same way as Mr. Short's friend. I thought to myself,

What should I look for and do? I don't know and I am terrified.

I survived this introduction to the consulting world, and thrived on the creative and problem solving aspects of my job. Creative Universal seemed like a perfect place for me. The Ford project was in the late development stage and the production of training materials and rollout of classroom seminars across the U.S. and Canada were on the horizon. Within weeks I felt a hypomanic mood coming on, and as a result I saw, said, and did things my co-workers questioned. An example of it was an event in a meeting room filled with instructional designers, artists, and production people. While they busily chewed on issues and tossed around possible solutions, I slowly and deftly built a solution in my mind.

Because I'm a ruminative thinker I create pictures in my head, similar to visualizing all the planets in the solar system. I can then move and rotate the problem around, like they're in orbit, so it's easy for me to look at a problem from many different directions. What I think I do is look from the viewpoints of others. In the end I select the choice with the best chance of success for everyone and then share it with my coworkers. Unfortunately, the initial reception to my solution is quite often negative and while my suggestions are usually plausible… all the left brain, detail, and procedural thinkers demand to know the steps I used to solve the problem. I'm sorry, there are none; they exist only in the deepest, intuitive recesses of my mind.

While I can quickly create solutions, I simply cannot explain the "how" in the detail they require. Frequently, two or three weeks later my doubters will finish their own analysis, find elements of my solution acceptable, and incorporate them in their own plan.

While at Creative Universal, one of my associates at Clark Equipment called me. He had bad news. All of the people I had worked with at Clark were greeted that Monday morning with a chain locking the doors of the building, and a note "All employees assigned to work in this building please report to the HR Department." It was the last day of work for everyone in the building.

It was in my third month at my new job in Detroit when the last, fatal layoff occurred at Clark, and they moved their operations to Korea. One thing is for sure, when I tell people what I see, what I think, and what I'm doing, they often don't believe me. They look at me like I'm living out on the fringes, but I've learned it takes fortitude not to give up on my personal convictions, and experience keeps reminding me to trust myself. I may have a mental disorder, but relieving myself of the stress caused by constant conflict has helped me gain confidence.

HYPOMANIC VS. DEPRESSIVE

1985

———— ✦ ————

USING OBSERVATION AND feedback skills, I've learned to determine when my behavior is hypomanic . . . by monitoring its intensity.

When I'm merely making a point, listeners think I'm cramming it down their throats.

When I'm speaking forcefully, listeners think I'm raging and screaming.

When I'm excited, listeners think I'm berserk.

And, when I'm emotionally involved in what I'm saying, listeners think I'm scary and dangerous.

It can take as long as a week for me to recognize these behaviors and attitudes because the behavior cycles change slowly, like a swinging pendulum from hypomanic to depressive as in the following chart.

HYPOMANIC to DEPRESSIVE

Strong	to	Weak
Confident	to	Self-absorbed
Loud	to	Soft-spoken
Aggressive	to	Passive
Enthusiastic	to	Uninterested

Experience has taught me that self-absorbed, the opposite of confidence, is a dangerous place for me to reside. It's a place where my mind and body are disconnected from the real world, in a cozy state of isolation. Picture a house in flames as the fire truck roars toward the fire with siren screaming. Inside, you could find me calmly sitting on the floor, surrounded by flames. Mesmerized, I would follow the colors and patterns created by the dancing flames, oblivious to the danger around me.

However, when you interrupt me from this cocoon state, expect an explosion of irritation and anger. You've just broken a spell that let me quiet my mind. You've introduced the reality I was escaping. You just ruined everything!

Over these many years, I've developed some clues to know when I'm displaying hypomanic behavior. Mainly it has to do with the speed of my brain processing. For example:

The more manic I am, the dumber you look to me. (I'm thinking really fast).

I become irritable because you can't keep up with me. You talk too slow, and I want to finish your sentences. I can, you know (while in this state of mind).

Quit interrupting me! I have images in my head that your interruption destroyed, just to answer one stupid question of yours. Do you know how much work it is to rebuild that vision and go back to where I was? If you did, then you'd leave me alone!

Why can't you see images like I do?

Why don't you understand? It's so simple. No, I haven't got time to explain it to you. I'm in a hurry.

Not knowing what my mood or behavior will be at any point in time, my anxiety increases, depending on the number of people I'm with. Given my fear of inappropriate behavior or a hypomanic mood, it's no wonder I'm exhausted after an evening with a crowd. Trying to avoid this uneasiness by isolating myself, close friends say I appear aloof. But then, when I deliberately sit with only one or two people in a social setting, I'm told I appear anti-social.

I do this intentionally to protect myself. Never knowing what mood I'll be in, I can't trust my actions, and need to minimize my social exposure. What's normal for me can be over the top for others.

Then there's the hard-to-define line between what is considered Bipolar behavior and just an ordinary personality trait. My current psychiatrist cautions me from time to time that not all of my behavior can be attributed to Bipolar disorder.

"Don," Dr. Mason said, "You still have a personality, and that personality is going to express itself. That doesn't mean that it's always stimulated by a Bipolar issue."

Oh, but dumb stuff happens to me, and when it does I want to blame my Bipolar disorder. There's got to be a way to tell the difference, but I'm never quite sure how to do that. About the only barometer I have to tell the difference is the frequency of a behavior.

If I'm overly chatty, talking fast, sharing ideas one-a-minute, and dominating the conversation at a table of eight people, I could be displaying hypomanic behavior. If I notice this behavior, then I try to observe whether the behavior continues the next day or two. If it seems to be just a singular event, then reluctantly I try to accept the fact that it's just a part of my personality, not Bipolar disorder.

Navigating through such experiences is so new to me I'm not very good at it, yet. Only within the past two years have I become aware there's a personality element that's not a part of this mental disorder. I still can only recognize and evaluate the matter days later, through what I call my rear view mirror.

My Rearview Mirror

1985

I am the fool whose life's been spent
Between what's said and what is meant.[17]

⸺ ◆ ⸺

IN SPITE OF all I've said about my behavior in groups and the clues I've learned, I still don't recognize the effects of my behavior on the specific day it occurs. For some reason, what's filtered from my awareness in real time becomes vividly apparent to me in retrospect. Oftentimes it ruins my day.

This "behavior" thing is not just confusing, it makes me angry. If I'm Bipolar why do I also have to deal with this mystery?

What I understand is that Bipolar disorder has sharp spikes up into mania, followed by a spike down into

---

[17]©Carrie Newcomer Music, Admin. BMG Chrysalis.

depression. But not me! I seem to be wallowing in the mud all the time, never seeing a spike anywhere.

My God! Why is it so hard to realize the effects of what I'm doing today until tomorrow, when it's too late to make changes? Why do I have to learn today what I did yesterday to make a fool of myself, offend, or embarrass someone?

It's deeply painful to repeatedly move through the cycle of embarrassment, shame, remorse, and guilt, and know it's far too late to take corrective action. If I had to pull all my regrets behind me, I'd look like an ant dragging a bag of popcorn.

I was convinced that I had overcome whatever caused the incident at the party I mentioned earlier, that made my former wife so irate. Imagine my dismay when the same thing happened on a vacation Pat and I shared in downtown San Diego. As I recalled, we visited the zoo, went whale watching, and took an evening walking tour of the old city—just a lot of nice experiences. When we got home my wife was very upset about my behavior in San Diego. She said she had to bite her tongue numerous times to avoid saying something in public.

How depressing. My mood went flat as a pancake.
I remember a wonderful time, just like the party with my first wife, and again I didn't see any signs that I behaved inappropriately. It's devastating. Why can't I recognize what I am doing?

By now you know how much I care about Pat and letting her down was a great disappointment. Perhaps, I had assumed it was safe to relax and drop my guard when with my wife. Obviously, that isn't true. It seems apparent to me that I need to utilize my observation skills around her as well. And, when with her... I need to be as sensitive about my hypomanic and depressive behavior as I am with anyone else.

As you can well imagine, the unexpected repercussions from these random reactions are maddening. I worry about it all the time. Incidents like these only heighten my fear of being offensive. That's why I relish any time alone, because it's the only place I can truly let my mind relax.

Knowing these things about my behavior, I make every effort to prepare myself for the way I want to behave at any given event. Then, in the moment, imagine my dismay to find that I have absolutely no control over my behavior. My chorus practice is a good example. I usually pop off with a wisecrack in an effort to be humorous and break any tension I'm feeling.

"Please, people. Hold your books up and watch me," the director said.

We sing a page of music, and then the pianist fumbled. "I'm sorry," he said, "but I'm having trouble seeing you."

"Well," I interrupt, "just pick up the piano and watch the director like the rest of us."

The chorus laughed, the director shook her head and sighed in exasperation.

I have been told that my wisecracks annoy some people, so before practice I make an effort to be calm, quiet, and make a commitment to not interrupt the rehearsal. I'm confident I can do that. But, all of a sudden, here I am, wise-cracking and tossing sarcastic comments around like a young boy tossing around a baseball. I don't know why it happens; I'm the guy who's supposedly trying to stay in the background.

Unfortunately, sarcasm shows up in my rear-view mirror, too. It's another one of those things I'm not aware of when it's happening. Although I think my little quips are cute, I've learned that my primary form of humor is sarcasm. I don't know why I feel the need to be humorous. I don't even tell jokes very well. I sense it's a way to deflect attention from myself, which is crazy because it just brings attention back to me, like a huge, beaming search light.

You'd think it would occur when I'm in an awkward situation where I'm nervous and uncomfortable. But that's not true. These outbursts of ill-timed and inappropriate humor happen during those times when I'd prefer to keep a low profile behind the crowd in the back of the room. Obviously, this sarcasm contributes to my social problems, but I don't know how to stop it.

What I've said and done have created some rather serious consequences. I've lost friends on at least three different occasions without ever knowing why. When I say "lost" I mean just that. I never see or hear from them again. They never answer the phone if I call, never send a Christmas card, nothing. Once we invited a couple I'd known for years to our home for dinner, and the next day they vanished. I haven't a clue what I said or what I did to stimulate their reaction, but it's been years without any contact at all.

This fear I feel is like a two-edged sword. On one side are the repercussions from my behavior. On the other side is the remorse I feel for offending someone. In each case I feel guilt first, then remorse. I anxiously want to fix what I've caused, but I can't. So I remain helpless to the shame that pulls me into the depths of depression.

I absolutely hate it. This cycle is why I work so hard to anticipate problems, control my behavior and walk away from trouble. Imagine just how exhausting this mental process is. The reason I try to have contact with as few people as possible, is to minimize my exposure to negative reactions, and those dreaded images in my rear view mirror.

"Never forget that the person with Bipolar disorder does not have control of his/her mood state. Those of us who do not suffer from a mood disorder sometimes expect mood-disorder patients to be able to exert the same control over their emotions and behavior that we ourselves are able to.

But, you can only exert self-control if the control mechanisms are working properly, and in people with mood disorders, they are not."[18]

Without outside help from family or friends, I'm the last one to know my behavior is out of line. My rearview mirror serves me well—unfortunately, it's always too late.

_____

[18] Bipolar Disorder, 2014, Francis Mark Mondimore, M.D., Johns Hopkins School of Medicine

MADDENING MATRIX

1985

———◆———

MY APARTMENT IN Warren, Michigan, was only ten minutes from the office. I put as much effort into settling in and decorating as I did with the one I left in Kalamazoo. I felt calm and comfortable in my new apartment. The only connections remaining in Kalamazoo were my psychiatrist, my divorce attorney, and Pat.

I would see Pat when I returned to Kalamazoo, but she didn't come to Detroit. I enjoyed visiting her to get away from Detroit now and then.

Creative Universal utilized a matrix organization system, which meant there would be a new group of people for every project. Typical meetings included group representatives from illustrations, text processing, marketing, motor vehicle, accounting, and my training group.

With this many people in one meeting, the chances of my behavior being inappropriate or questioned by somebody were constant. My fear of disclosure was amplified. My eyes would

125

search a meeting room trying to read each participant's reactions to me for signs my behavior might be inappropriate. This intense stress caused me to sweat under my arms until it went through my shirt and suit coat. One day a co-worker asked if I was okay, because my face was so flushed.

How embarrassing.

I'd return home exhausted, but I cherished the days I'd have to travel and miss those meetings.

When our divorce was final, February 1986, my share of the proceeds from selling a house, a car, and investments was far less than I had hoped. Sixty percent of my share went to my divorce attorney, leaving me with just enough for a down payment on a modest house. Thank God I had a company car, or it wouldn't have been possible. It was so nice to live in a place with more than three rooms. I felt a sense of freedom as well as some stability in my life.

Of course, with the new home and the growing success of the Ford project at work, my enthusiasm shifted once more to hypomania. I pursued ideas, created plans, managed projects, and achieved goals. Right up my alley . . . except for the impatience and irritability.

Again, I'm hypomanic. I'm thinking fast and people around me are just irritating the hell out of me. They're thinking and talking soooo slow.

They are caught up in the steps of the procedure and make me want to cry, "Just give me the baby, damn it! I don't need to hear about the labor pains!"

With every up there's a down, and my hypomania never lasts forever. Depression usually follows. And so I crashed. After all, I had just expended a tremendous amount of energy and that led to fatigue.

Ever cognizant of my potential behavior, it is far too easy to be cocooned within my depressive shell; I become self-absorbed, resist interruptions that break my spell, or require answers to questions. Even worse are surprises or requests that demand my physical attention. Like the proverbial cornered rat, I snip and snarl and sometimes explode at an intruder.

I fear each moment this will happen. Hypomanic or depressive, bad things can happen to me at any moment—and never of my choosing!

The following example perfectly reflects how an unexpected emotion surprised me.

While teaching seminars in Canada, one of my employees wasn't paying attention and sent me the wrong student manuals for the dealership service advisor's seminar. Of course, I was forced to improvise and create ways to teach the seminar without the proper materials. The next day I suffered the pain and embarrassment of apologizing to their bosses for the mix up and lack of proper training materials.

My return flight home from Canada was the third day I had fumed over the stress and embarrassment I endured. I couldn't wait to fire the culprit. The next morning I met with the employee, in my secretary's presence, and fired him.

However, in the process of explaining why, my pent up feelings exploded, and I went into a screaming rage. I wasn't aware until afterward when my secretary commented, "Well, I learned one thing… to never make you mad." Totally unaware of my outrageous behavior until she spoke, her statement jarred me out of my trance and back into reality. I was totally unaware of what I had just done. I was also filled with unbelievable shame and embarrassment.

A New Start

1986

———◆———

ALTHOUGH I WORKED with many young and attractive women in the fast-paced consulting business, I still felt most comfortable with Pat. A warm, friendly, sociable person… she is everything I am not. We seemed to fit well together. However, I didn't want to repeat the same situation that happened with my former wife and me. If Pat was going to have a negative reaction about my illness, I wanted it to be before we thought of making any commitments.

It took some time for me to find the courage to reveal my "secrets" with her. I had guarded my illness from others for so many years. I worried that telling her could cut the cord between us quickly. But eventually I found the courage to tell her about my Bipolar disorder. Surprisingly, her concern about this new information turned to acceptance.

"You know," she said, "in all the time I've known you I haven't seen what you're describing. I think I'm okay with it."

Although immensely relieved, I was still cautious; I felt like I was telling her that I bought a new pet dog. She thought she understood, but could she? That dog wasn't in the house yet.

Like everything else I do in life, my plan to propose was strategic! I had the ring, and wanted to make my proposal something special. I invited Pat to come for a weekend visit. Knowing she always prefers to cook at home, I planned the event at my house. Not a cook myself, I thought the best thing would be to have the meal catered. My business associates knew a number of excellent caterers, and I booked one of their favorites. I hid the ring in the bouquet on the table.

I am ready, but is she?

I proposed. Pat accepted, and we were married the following November.

We relocated her to Detroit where she found a job working for a dentist. Things were going well and we were comfortable. It didn't bother her that I was assigned to do all of the sales and service advisor training work in Canada, but eventually it bothered me.

I spent forty-seven weeks of the next year traveling to and from Canada conducting sales meetings with owners of Ford dealerships, and training their service managers and service advisors. I'd see Pat only on weekends, leaving her in a strange city to fend for herself. She survived, of course, but I worried. I'd lost one marriage, and I didn't want my work to ruin this one.

The day I finished a seminar in Vancouver I rented a car and drove to Seattle to catch a domestic flight home. I can tell you that I was beyond tired and growing depressed as I drove through Seattle in the traffic and the smog. I looked out over the bay and saw a mirror image of Chicago.

Oh my God! I've been traveling for too many years.

When Pat picked me up at the Detroit airport, my mind was made up.

"Honey," I said, "I don't know what you're going to do with the rest of your life, but this is my last day consulting with Creative Universal."

"Do you know what you're going to do?" she asked.

"No, but I think we need to move back to your hometown so at least you're comfortable while I look for work."

I gave my notice the next day, we sold out and moved into an apartment in Kalamazoo while we looked for a house. When her old boss heard she was back in town he hired her immediately to fill the job she had left.

Awkward Success

1989

———— ◆ ————

A FORMER NEIGHBOR of mine heard I was in town and asked me, for the third time, to join him in the insurance sales business with Prudential. He had always thought I'd be good at it. There were no other opportunities at the time, and with his help I got hired. After the required training and licensing I became an insurance agent in a group of 30 other agents.

With enthusiasm bordering on hypomanic again, I became the top agent within six months. There was a lot of grumbling and backbiting from the group, but they weren't paying me so I ignored it. Questions were still raised about what I was doing and how I was doing it. How could I possibly surpass them?

How to succeed at the job hadn't been hard for me to figure out. The agents that smoked cigarettes and drank coffee while they bantered about this and that, were certainly no example. I figured if I were to be an insurance agent, I had to be the best I could be. I developed a plan to farm out the various parts of the job that were time consuming—cold calling and setting appointments—to a telemarketing group that solicited people in the income levels I wanted to meet. I located an office to work out of that didn't include 30 folks sitting around drinking coffee. I also lined up a secretary to manage the office. My intentions? To schedule more daytime office visits and spend fewer nights in people's homes.

The plans were made and ready. All I had to do was pull the trigger on the starting gun and the pieces of my new business plan would fall together. Thank God I didn't.

That next Saturday morning I walked into the branch office and was surprised to hear my branch manager telling six new agents everything I planned to do for my new office. Right down to the dime, including my rent for the building, the salary I planned to pay my secretary, how I used telemarketing, and my plan to eliminate night meetings in clients' homes.

I turned and left quietly before I caused a scene. Once in my car I exploded with fury. I ranted and raved about how I had been violated.

No one else, including the branch manager had the creativity to do what I did. No one else spent the time and energy to create what I did. He stole it! He took my creation and just gave it away.
It wasn't his to give away!

In my mind he was creating competition within his own branch that would hurt my business. I couldn't have it. On Monday morning Don Wooldridge, the branch manager's top salesman, resigned and walked out the door.

My friend in the office later shared with me that the regional manager visited soon after. The branch manager contacted me asking me to reconsider. Prudential called me about a job in Grand Rapids, Michigan. I interviewed with them, but subsequently refused their offer. Still furious that he stole my plans, I didn't shed a tear when three months after my resignation, Prudential fired the branch manager.

I've probably made it perfectly clear that when it comes to making decisions I am "all or nothing." If something is shitty, I can't force myself to see how playing with it is going to make anything better. Everything just gets messy and you still have to wash your hands. In this case my boss was threatening my livelihood, and stealing ideas from me. That gut instinct kicked in... I had to quit; there was simply no reason to work for an individual I couldn't trust.

Can you believe Pat understood and supported my decisions? It confirmed my belief I had married the right woman.

SECTION III

CHANGING
COURSE

CHANGING COURSE

1990

———— • ————

HAVE YOU EVER wondered whether it is possible to be right and wrong at the same time? The right part was that I could sell insurance successfully. The wrong part was that I didn't like it. Again, I had put myself in a situation that would require constant interpersonal communications. Worse yet, the job was steeped in rejection.

I learned the insurance business well. I earned numerous awards and a decent income. I did the job well, but it was as uncomfortable as a pair of shoes that pinch your toes. In time I became aware that I'd made another bad career choice. Twice in a row.

How in the world can I possibly look for another job and know it's right for me? I am filled with fear and afraid to move forward. I need help!

After some thought I turned to the owners of Psychological Associates in St. Louis, Missouri. I'd worked with them for a number of years and was successful as a certified instructor for one of their weeklong management courses. Many times the President, Dr. Lefton, had shared with me the good results stemming from their out placement testing program. I felt that's exactly what I needed.

Dr. Lefton was more than willing to have me go through their outplacement testing, but he thought a group based only 90 minutes away in Lansing, Michigan, would be as good and less expensive for me. He called Plant-Moran and helped set up a three-day test.

Over those three days I took abstract and concrete intelligence tests, worked through word games, personality tests, aptitude tests, and a test of thinking patterns, and puzzles. I liked solving the puzzles.

Quite simply, if I'm hypomanic I can look at those ten colored puzzle blocks for a second or two and see the pattern. Within a minute I'm finished assembling them. Piece of cake. However, if I am depressed, I can look at those puzzle pieces for twenty minutes and still not know what to do with them. I guess that's the easiest way to demonstrate my brain speed and visualization when I'm hypomanic, and just how dull my brain is when I'm depressed.

A week or so later I returned to meet with a counselor and review the results. No surprise... suitable jobs did not include consulting or insurance sales! Property management was my strength. Preferably outside physical and/or mechanical work. My thoughts immediately took me back all those years to the millwright job I turned down when I was 18 years old.

Interesting, Don! You had the opportunity then, to do what outplacement testing now recommends.

Intelligence? It isn't concrete intelligence that's useful in consulting or insurance work. Although I had the talent to do the corporate jobs I held over the years, they were not well suited to me, emotionally. Policies, procedures, and frequent interpersonal communications are my weakness, yet I kept getting sucked into that line of work. In retrospect I am quite sure I never realized what I was doing to myself.

**This whole process and understanding leaves me feeling so damned stupid! How many years have I spent...
doing absolutely the wrong thing for my mental health?
Twenty-eight to be exact.**

I learned my strength is concrete intelligence, like the machine service work I had done at John Deere and Clark Equipment in the past. The question stirred powerfully in my mind.

God, what am I to do with this piece of information? I certainly have a new direction, but no job. What next?

I developed a plan to interview local people in every aspect of property management. I met with landscapers, realtors, and golf course maintenance superintendents. I found the golf course maintenance business interested me the most because it's the most visual. Another strength of mine.

I needed education to do this, so I contacted Michigan State University. I was accepted, but their criteria required I work on a golf course maintenance crew for a full year before I could start. Age forty-four is not a good time to be returning to college and making a significant career change. Ah, the power of confidence... I felt I had the best information about myself I'd ever had, trusted it, and took the plunge.

I sacrificed my company car and previous income of $60,000, and worked on the maintenance crew of a local golf course for $5 per hour. The lesson I quickly learned is that in the Midwest there is no such thing as a forty-hour week. The storms of the spring and summer shorten work days, as do the frosts of fall. I soon began looking for ways to finish this one- year requirement, and focused on Arizona.

My mother and father were living in the Phoenix area, and the weather provided the work that I needed during the winter months. The people at Michigan State University helped me by contacting a golf course superintendent in Scottsdale, Arizona who was an MSU graduate. That's where I sent my resume. Seeing my experience and qualifications, he passed it on to another golf course superintendent nearby, who interviewed me on the phone and offered me a job for $8 per hour.

Starting October, 1991 our family was geographically split once again; Pat stayed in Michigan and continued to work at the dentist's office while I went to Arizona for six months. I moved into the second bedroom of my parent's apartment. Each day I drove fifty miles one-way to work at Desert Mountain, where I started at the bottom of the ladder as a laborer, and did menial physical jobs.

The first thing I noticed was that fifty-four of the sixty employees were Hispanic. To me that meant if I was going to work with them, I needed to learn Spanish. Fortunately, our irrigator wanted to learn English, so we started a "word-a-day" game. Eventually it led to clocks, then calendars, then reading the newspaper. I planned to take a Spanish class the following year at the local community college.

The most important development for me was that physical work outdoors was just what I needed. Believe it or not, being physically tired had a positive impact on my mental issues. Also, golf course maintenance is an extremely visual endeavor which suited me to a tee.

Secondly, I learned that this particular club provided uniforms, medical benefits, and two week vacations. Third, the superintendent informed me that I didn't need to go to Michigan State for two years like I had planned; he showed me how I could attend the winter program at Rutgers University in New Jersey. Only ten weeks a year for two years and I'd be just as qualified. It was obvious that golf in Arizona was a serious business, and if I was going to be a part of it I needed to seriously consider Arizona.

PULLING UP STAKES

1992

———— • • ————

PAT FLEW TO Phoenix for a week over the Christmas holiday. While we were together I shared that I had not experienced either hypomania or depression since I arrived in Arizona. We also spent time talking about our future. She agreed that the obvious answer was to relocate to Arizona, especially because the Rutgers University program took less money and time away from the job, than the two full years at Michigan State. When she left she was prepared to put our house on the market and start the moving process.

The house sold at absolutely the wrong time; Desert Mountain was hosting a televised Senior's PGA Golf Tournament. We started preparations mid-January and were working sixteen hours a day the last week of March during the tournament. I asked about getting some time off, but the best I could do was to fly out April 1, after we prepped the course for the last day of play. Pat sold the house and faxed papers for me to sign. With the help of her son, she rented a U-Haul truck and car hauler and loaded everything. When I arrived April 1st everything was done and the truck packed. The next

145

day Pat and I drove the rig back to the Arizona apartment I had rented for us.

About two months later the corporate agronomist asked me to meet in his office. I had never met with him before, and worried I'd done something wrong. Cautiously I entered his office. It surprised me that the meeting wasn't about me. "What's your wife doing these days?" he asked. Well, she had a part-time job, so I told him about it. "I have an urgent matter to resolve," he said. "Do you think she could come see me tomorrow?" She could, and did, and was hired as an administrative assistant at Renegade maintenance, one of the three courses on the property. Seventeen years later she retired, to the disappointment of everyone with whom she worked.

BLACKOUTS

1994

———— • • ————

BY 1992 I had enough experience to take the Arizona state pesticide applicator test. My boss and other supervisors were surprised that I passed the licensing test on the first try. They all had taken it at least twice to pass.

By 1994 I had two years' experience applying pesticides. On this particular day we were testing a growth regulator around the edges of the greens, called the collars. Every week I'd make an application, and on this particular day we were doing the same.

After loading the sprayer, I put the chemical bottle alongside the tank so I could mix the next load out on the course. We sprayed the collars as usual until I ran out of chemical on the tenth green. Turning to retrieve the chemical bottle and mix the next load, I froze. I thought my eyes were deceiving me. Holding a bottle of Round-Up, a chemical that kills grass and weeds, I tried to comprehend the fact that I'd just sprayed ten greens with a grass killer, not the growth regulator.

How could this happen? I had done everything the same as other days. Andres, who was helping me, backed away holding his hands up like the sheriff had a gun in his back, "No problem for me, amigo!"

"I know, I know." I said. "Come on, we've gotta hurry."

Disturbed about what had happened to me, my next action was clear. I had to be honest, and inform the superintendent quickly. Easy to say but hard to do. With my mind spinning and felling like a cannon just blew a hole in my stomach.

I went right to the superintendent's office and told him what I'd done and where we had sprayed. I sat in the office, like a naughty schoolboy, and waited while the superintendent ordered any number of potential corrective actions. In the end, none of them worked. Waiting for him to return, I sat in dismay and pondered what had just happened.

Is this another blackout incident—just like the night with Mr. Short's client and friend?

Why wasn't I aware of what I was doing? In my mind I had the right chemical; in my mind I mixed and applied it correctly; but, in reality it didn't happen that way.

**Why? I can see. I can touch. I can think.
I know what to do. Why did this happen to me?**

I sat alone embarrassed and confused, especially because there hadn't been any mood swings, lately. I'd had a good run of being as emotionally stable and normal as my personality would allow.

I don't understand... what happened?

I could see no reason I wouldn't be fired, and I wondered how to tell Pat. Even worse, after I was fired, she'd be the one to hear the story and questions over and over again.

The corporate agronomist is the man who saved my job for me. First, neither he nor the superintendent could quarrel with the fact that I was honest and responded so quickly instead of trying to hide the mistake. He subsequently met with the golf pro to discuss the unfortunate incident, shuffled the budget and implemented a previously approved project to immediately replace the collars. For all the golf club members knew, burning the collars on the greens was a part of the process.

I kept my job and Pat only heard what she already knew from employees around the property. But the Hispanic workers weren't fooled. Oh, no. I knew all of them, and they were merciless. There wasn't a day while we worked overtime replacing those collars on the greens that they didn't tease me or cuss me for killing the greens. They called me "El Muerto," meaning "The Death."

One major thing I lost was the club's tuition refund plan that would have helped me pay for my schooling at Rutgers. A big loss for us financially, but certainly understandable.

None of the doctors who have treated my Bipolar disorder have ever discussed these blackouts—each of which had the potential to end my career. If I'd have been fired, there's no way I'd ever have gotten a job on a golf course again. If a top 100 golf course fired me for misuse of chemical, the word would spread like wildfire. As it happened, superintendents on the East Coast knew about it before the week was over, anyway. Needless to say, my fear escalated; afraid of when the next one would happen. Stress? Fatigue? I don't know. I just know something caused my mind to go blank.

BAD JUDGMENT

1997

———◆———

MY FIRST WINTER semester at Rutgers University in New Jersey, I stayed in a hotel located in New Brunswick—the city was so noisy I had to buy earplugs in order to sleep. They came in handy for studying too, since the police sirens seemed to be on a timer, as did the medical helicopters flying low onto the hospital pad near-by. Busses and cars honking filled any gaps. Add to that the snowiest winter in twenty-five years— that's how I started my ten-week session in Golf Turf Management.

I arrived from sunny, peaceful Arizona, and found New Jersey disturbing at many levels. The dark sky instantly put a damper on my mood. Depressed, I didn't go anywhere that I didn't have to be; the noise helped keep me in my shell. Then came the Friday night dances in the hotel's ballroom that led to fights, gunfire, and knifings. All of this occurred directly beneath my window.

The final straw for me was a police raid on hotel residents selling drugs. Imagine my angst as the police chased the perpetrators up and down the hallways, until they caught and arrested them all.

I chose to bury myself in the books to avoid the streets of New Brunswick. At age 51, it was especially important that I do well, because my competition for jobs back home would be against younger men half my age. I would have to prove myself beyond a doubt to have a chance for a job.

Numerous classmates staying in the hotel vowed not to return to the hotel next year. I went with them as we scouted apartments where we could team up to keep our living costs reasonable. As luck would have it, we found one not far from campus, and reserved the apartments before going home.

These new housing arrangements made the start of our second session much more bearable. Being a part of the group of guys helped me stay out of depression. We worked hard, but had some fun, too. I felt much better during our second year classes. However, the gray skies remained and I did suffer mild depression, but nothing that hindered my success at school. At the graduation ceremony I received my certificate with honors.

I was proud of my accomplishment and anxious to take on management responsibility. Unfortunately, that would not happen at Desert Mountain. The policy would not allow husband and wife to work in the same department. And, the job opening that I wanted to apply for was at the golf course where my wife worked. There was no hope for me to continue at Desert Mountain in any kind of management position.

Not wanting to get sidetracked in my quest to use my degree, I diligently worked on the Desert Mountain Maintenance crew while I looked for an assistant superintendent's position.

I barely got started when one of my former superintendents called. Turf grow-in was starting on a new, near-by golf course, and he needed an assistant superintendent. Because I did what I said I would do back in 1991 (finishing my education) he wanted me to work for him. With that, I began work in Fountain Hills, Arizona. On my first day he says, "Don, I want you to do your job like this is your golf course."

It was hard work. A lot had to be done while keeping track of contractors as well. Twelve-hour days were normal, and as spring became summer, the days grew hotter. When the rent for our Scottsdale apartment increased, we moved to a duplex in Fountain Hills, which shortened both of our drives to work.

Continually challenged by new experiences, my moods stayed steady. I had both disappointments and successes, but my moods remained unexpectedly resilient. Nothing stayed with me more than a day or two. I was older than everybody on the crew, including my boss, but it didn't seem to be an issue. I tried very hard to make sure it wasn't.

I especially liked the visual feedback I received from nature; the course grew as we shaped dirt to plant and grow vast expanses of grass. It felt good to be outdoors during the summer months, even though I babysat new greens when temperatures were above 115 degrees. The new sod required even closer attention so it didn't burn out and I embraced how apparent it was that this was where I needed to be, instead of corporate offices.

Then I did something stupid! The development company had a performance evaluation system called the 360 review. Each person being evaluated would have both superiors and subordinates respond to their performance. My boss's turn came up. He was tough and eccentric, but worst of all he drank beer in his truck while on the job. We all knew it, so the mechanic and irrigator said they were going to include it on their review, they encouraged me to do the same. As I would soon learn, apparently, I was the only one who did. Two or three weeks later my boss drove up in his truck, "Hop in, we're going for a ride."

I got in his truck and didn't think much of it, since it happened frequently. We didn't go far, though, when he pulled into the clubhouse parking lot and stopped.

"Come on," he said, "I need to stop in the clubhouse for a minute."

Standing among the merchandise racks, I looked for new shirts as I waited for him to come out of the golf pro's office.

Instead, he opened the door halfway and asked, "Don, would you join me for a minute?"

I was of the opinion that important stuff must happen at the clubhouse, and intuition surfaced, making me guardedly curious about what I was walking into.

I was shocked when I saw the Vice President of Golf Course Operations sitting behind the desk. He was not a person that spent any time with me. I sat in a chair beside Ron, then looked up as the VP spoke, "It has come to my attention, Don, that you are trying to take over the maintenance of this golf course from Ron."

What? Where did that idea come from?

I took a deep breath before saying, "I'm sorry if you have that impression sir, but it certainly is not my intent."

"Well, that's how it appears. I want to tell you here and now that it's within my authority to select the maintenance superintendent for Sun Ridge Canyon, and I selected Ron for the job, not you.

Why am I being accused of something I didn't do, and not even aware of?

I turned to Ron and asked, "Do you seriously believe that I'm trying to take over this golf course from you?"

"That's why we're here," Ron replied.

He does. Why? He's saying this to get rid of me.

"Well, I think I've made myself clear," the VP added. "As of now, Don, your services are no longer needed at Sun Ridge Canyon. Ron's going to keep you working while you look for a job, but understand, you need to leave as soon as possible.

I was devastated. I liked living in the same town and loved the golf course. Obviously, I had gotten suckered into trouble. Although my history was filled with the ability to be quick to anticipate most things, there were others, like this one, that I had missed entirely. Getting another job on a golf course didn't happen. Every time I'd have an opportunity Ron would intercept their calls, and I would never get an interview.

My judgment has been terrible.
Now I am feeling really down and disappointed.
I need help, and I know it!

POOR CHOICES

1998

━━━ • ━━━

ALTHOUGH I DIDN'T know what the Mundus Institute was, that's where I found a job. It seemed almost perfect. Mundus, which is a private golf academy, attracted and trained golf course managers, pros, and maintenance students.

I felt lucky to find any job in the golf industry after so many rejections by golf course maintenance superintendents. The owner thought I had the perfect experiences, including course maintenance, new course construction, education from Rutgers and lots of teaching experience. I made more money than I did at the golf course, although it didn't provide benefits, vacation or sick time. Not even time off for Christmas. But, I had a job. How could I complain?

The prospects were exciting—I was able to teach again! A perfect opportunity. My enthusiasm peaked once again into hypomania as I began teaching, and spent months of out-of-class-time updating all the old lesson plans left behind.

I even introduced field trips that illustrated the topics we were studying. Surprise! The very golf course superintendents who previously refused to hire me were more than supportive when I inquired about my class visiting their course on a field trip.

I finished my first year and started my second with the new materials and activities I'd created, but I began to wear down. Imagine my dismay as over time I became aware that eighty percent of my students didn't give a damn. They included managers and golf pros who were required to take my class for their diploma. The topics in my curriculum were relevant to only twenty percent of my class, but I still had to put up with the behavior of the uninterested masses.

The joy I first envisioned in the job turned to bitterness, as more and more I began to feel like a puppet. The negativity wore on me and I started to resent my role in the institute. Depressed and disillusioned I simply went through the motions, and began looking for another job. One consideration was the lack of time off, especially at Christmas, which felt awkward for Pat and me as well.

The opportunity I needed to shift to a healthier state of mind opened up in the landscaping industry. A landscape company in south Scottsdale, who needed an experienced field supervisor, hired me. My life improved immediately, as did the benefits package of medical, vacation and holiday time off. The pay was also better and included a company truck as well.

The regional manager liked my background and wanted me to learn and grow into the branch manager position. Obviously, a job with a future intrigued me. Unfortunately, my co-workers didn't like the idea.

Here I am again, employed by an operation that needs my skill at rebuilding. How do I find these jobs anyway?

I found the two supervisors who still worked there intentionally annoying. I worked in a bullpen environment with these two older and more seasoned supervisors and tried to be effective, efficient, and manage my crews well. Unfortunately, my co-workers didn't want me to do anything differently from what they were doing. Anytime I didn't comply with their expectations, they interfered with both my work and my crews.

The loss of tools had gotten way out of hand. The regional manager liked my idea of a tool crib where tools were checked out in the morning and back in after work. Taking on the challenge, I supervised the building of a tool crib, the numbering system, and method to check tools in and out. After the orientation of all employees on the new system, we started, and then… I began losing tools.

As time passed I found that the two supervisors I worked with were taking tools out of the crib without checking them out and passing them along to their crews. Do you ever find the behavior of others as downright unbelievable?

As I became more effective, and my crews obviously performed better than my co-worker's, they retaliated again.

They thought it would be funny to send me on a wild goose chase into Scottsdale during rush hour traffic, so they told me "one of their guys" had seen "one of my guys" on the city street with a broken down 5-gang mower. They urged me to get up there right away. Of course, "their informer" had gone home already, so it was their word only. As my gut instinct kicked in, I considered the procedure that every mower must fill up at the gas station on Thomas Rd. before bringing the mower into the yard.

So I left the office, to the strains of their laughter of course, and drove a short mile to the gas station. I asked to see our company receipts, sorted through them and found that my mower operator filled up his machine 15 minutes earlier. Imagine how I surprised the conspirators when I got back to the office just minutes later. I sure didn't get any credit for being smart, but it was a pleasure to wipe the smiles off their faces.

Why is it that I can love my job, but not tolerate the office environment?

Unfortunately, my behavior mirrored that of the two older supervisors, but not that of a future branch manager. Although I was doing a good job, what once felt like a bright, shining future opportunity began to grow dim.

MORE CONFLICT

1998

———— ✦ ————

WORKING ABOUT EIGHT months through this experience as a branch manager trainee, I was really enjoying the job. Much better than golf course maintenance—probably because of the variety of properties and contact with the owners and my crews. Anyway, I was having fun when my wife's boss, Shawn, called from Desert Mountain.

"Don," he said, "I need you on my staff to help me."

There had been some inspections on the property, and the insurance and safety consultants told him he needed someone to clean up this mess, and Shawn fingered me.

"Shawn," I said, "thanks for the compliment, but I've got a good job and I like it."

"I know, I know. I've talked to Pat," Shawn said. "But I can pay you a lot more than you're making doing landscaping.

Think it over, and let me know what it would take for you to move up here and be my risk and training manager."

Think it over? Damn! I don't want to change jobs now.

I talked it over with Pat, and we agreed the best way to get out of it was to make my requirements so over the top Shawn couldn't possibly take them seriously. So I added 25% to my current salary, and demanded two weeks' vacation to replace what I would lose by changing jobs. Oh, and since I had a truck, I would demand to have a company truck, too.

It wasn't long before Shawn called again. I told him of my requirements, thinking I was really laying it on, and he said, "Is that it?"

"Yes, that's it," I said. "Fine, you're hired!"

Ohhhhh Shit! That's really not what I wanted?

RISK AND SAFETY TRAINING

1998

———— • ————

BECAUSE THERE ARE times I have been able to leave behind my fear and embrace the possibilities, I experience life shifts, and thus found myself a Risk and Safety Training Manager.

What the hell is that?

I personally was actually very well qualified as a "risk" because of the greens collars I'd burned, remember? But, I knew the property well, and took on the self-education and work with liability insurance adjusters, fire department inspectors, OSHA safety conferences, etc. to get a solid grip on the job. By the end of the year everything complied with all safety requirements. I had developed formal inspection categories, checklists existed for each of the six maintenance facilities, and was truly cooking right along when we hit a snag in finding labor. That changed everything.

Traditionally our labor force is Hispanic. The facility is located twenty to thirty miles away from Phoenix, in the Desert Mountain community in Scottsdale, Arizona, where homes are valued in multi-million dollars. The crisis in hiring and keeping labor was stimulated by the construction of many high-end golf courses between Phoenix and Desert Mountain. For the same wage, skilled labor didn't have to spend as much time and travel as it took to work for us. The most serious issue was hefty transportation costs. That was where Shawn's big idea came into play.

"Don, I want you to create a bussing system for our employees," Shawn declared.

"Why are you telling me, Shawn? Bussing isn't my job.

I'm the risk and safety training manager, remember?"

"Well, let me tell you something," he said. "Labor is my biggest risk, and if we don't get employees to work, you won't have a job. So build us a bussing system to get and keep our labor force."

"Shawn, I don't know anything about bussing. Are you sure you've got the right guy?"

Shawn had the final say. "Hell, I don't either. But that's what I've got you for. Go figure it out."

I shared Shawn's forward thinking and big picture scope of problem solving. We understood each other well on that score. But, I didn't have a good feeling about this bussing project. To me it felt like growing in a beautiful green lawn. Once in place, you have to mow it and fertilize it, etc. forever. Fear raised its nasty head and I could just feel an overpowering sense of dread. Once that bus is purchased, just who's going to keep track of where it is? My thoughts wouldn't let go; there had to be a way!

Ok, Don. You claim to be the man of challenges and solutions, just how are you going to manage this one?

To start, I scouted around for places to buy used buses. At each location I'd listen and ask questions to learn about state regulations and how they effected our needs. In the end I bought two used, 26 passenger yellow school busses. What an accomplishment, I thought, from nothing to two busses.

But my sense of accomplishment was quickly shattered when I was told we could not have yellow busses in the community. "Paint them." Shawn said. Hurriedly I stopped delivery and asked the bus supplier to paint them for us.

Not to be deterred from being the great solution provider, for the next couple of weeks I hustled around metro Phoenix. With all our employees' homes on a map I searched for appropriate bus stops. While I advertised and interviewed drivers I searched for a twenty-four-hour access storage facility to park and pick up our busses. Since timing is so essential to travel time in the Valley, I made practice runs from my proposed bus stops to Desert Mountain and back, before during and after work hours. I picked up busses, hired drivers, and installed two-way radios in my truck and both buses. That two-way radio in my truck became a steady, painful reminder of why I had not wanted this task from the beginning. It signaled with certainty that I was the "go-to" guy about every aspect of this bussing service for our employees.

When given a problem to solve like Shawn's staff transportation, it takes very little time between when I get into my head, visualize and create, and when I reach a hypomanic state. I just love to solve problems, which Shawn thoroughly understood, and I feed off the sight of the big picture and the small successes along the way. I'm always thrilled with the challenge; there is no obstacle I can't get over, under, or around.

Although I didn't want anything to do with busing, I did want to solve the problem. I wanted the problem, the challenge, and the thrill of completion. As I often do, however, more fear ultimately piled on and I paid an awfully high price for the thrill of this victory!

We removed the busses from storage at 3 a.m. to pick up riders at the bus stops an hour and a half before the 5 a.m. start times at Desert Mountain. Riders were picked up and returned to the bus stops before the busses were secured again at 4 p.m. Not surprisingly, I was told to be at the storage facility to ensure they were okay before their run, and again to secure them at the end of the day.

This is where the thrill of victory started to crumble. Living in east Phoenix I had to meet my drivers in north central Phoenix, about 50 miles away, making my day start at 2 a.m. and end around 5:30 p.m. (if traffic cooperated). Then Shawn became more demanding and I found myself physically drained. He wanted more monitoring and more reports to prove to management his idea was working. That's not what I wanted.

"Shawn, this is not my job. This isn't what you hired me for, remember? I'm supposed to be a risk and training manager, not a bus system babysitter! I want to do the job I was hired for. Find somebody to run this damn thing, and please just leave me out of it!"

I found myself repeating this conversation every few days until finally, one day as we rode together in a golf cart we stopped at the sixteenth hole. While we stood on the tee screaming at each other, three groups of employees quietly moved on to work on a different golf hole, staring at us like we were mad men.

As my fatigue built, I slid further into depression. My frustration increased until I became hypersensitive about absolutely everything. Every noise in the office affected me like those headaches, maybe you've had one, that amplified the sound of a pin drop until it vibrated in my head like a Chinese gong.

I want to scream!

Instead, I tell Shawn I can't stand the crowd and move my office to the basement of the clubhouse where I can have some privacy, peace, and quiet. It is the only way I can think to deal with the bus system.

I know Shawn and I still respect each other, but we are always going to disagree on these issues about busing employees. In my heart I know he has to and I know he realizes I don't want to do this anymore.

Although this pattern happened many times in my life, I begin to understand something about myself. I questioned just how many times I started something, but never finished. Just like this bussing project, I was on fire creating it, but bored to tears having to run it every day. The result: my being moody, angry, and wanting to avoid any day to day operations necessary to busing employees.

DEPRESSION

1999

———— • ————

I don't know how I started down this tailspin,
Why one more time I just did not see it coming.
And you'd think by now,
I'd figure out the pattern.[19]

I'M NO EXPERT Even medicated with an antidepressant, it still takes me three or four days to realize I'm depressed. A retrospective process, I have to look back over those days to recognize my inactivity. Like disregarding all projects or writing time and sitting for hours or lying down and sleeping. Deeper depression will find me rehashing my failings, guilt, or issues that have angered me in the past.

---

[19] ©Carrie Newcomer Music, Admin. BMG Chrysalis.

When I sense something's wrong, I've learned that I need to increase my antidepressant dosage by 10 mg or 20 mg. Even then, it'll take at least three days before I feel any improvement. Of course, when I do this, I call and leave a message for my doctor, telling him the symptoms I felt and how much I increased my dosage. Soon after I'll get a call from him either confirming my actions, or discussing my depression further and suggesting alternative actions.

Fear remains a part of my daily existence, even with the help of a psychiatrist and medication. I'm surprised depression occurs even though I'm faithful in taking my medication. However, I refuse to discontinue any dosages, fearful of what my moods and behavior would be like without them.

Fortunately my psychiatrist and I found the best antidepressant for me. The third one we tried was working, giving me control that didn't waver, and I remained stable over a number of months, which was great news.

Success meant my level of depression was more resilient, something I hadn't experienced before. I would experience normal depression and recover within a day or two. An incredible experience for me; I comprehended the different levels of depression, sufficiently to write about it.

If you look up the definition of "depression," you will find:

Depression: A condition of mental disturbance characterized by such feelings to a greater degree than seems warranted by the external circumstances; typically with lack of energy and difficulty in maintaining concentration or interest in life; despondency and dejection, typically felt over a period of time; and accompanied by feelings of hopelessness and inadequacy.

What a fine can of worms, this thing called depression! How do I arrive at this state of depression? Why do I stay there? And how do I get out?

There have been times in life when I've been so sensitive, the very slightest disappointment triggered depression. It was a quick, hard slide to a place that literally immobilized my thoughts and actions. During these episodes, my mind was in a stalemate with no idea where to go or how to get there. I simply stayed in this dark, lonely, fear-filled place.

It's clear to me when I am faced with these discomforting feelings: hopelessness and inadequacy, but to what degree am I hopeless or inadequate? I'm depressed, I am cognizant of that, but am I feeling 10 percent or 100 percent hopeless? And where on the barometer would the inadequacy measure? It is important to be able to determine whether what you are feeling is depression, and how severe it may be.

Have you ever had a day when you had the "blues?" Did you curl up in a chair and read a book until they went away? This is how I feel when hit with a mild level of depression. Have you totally lost interest in life and just curled up in bed and let the day go by? That's a more serious form of depression.

So how in the world would you know if you're seeing or feeling depression? We all have to have a way to anchor in our thoughts and feelings about particular things: the following poetic view of balloons is a perfect way to describe how I've experienced it.

The Full Balloon

We all know a full balloon is firm and bouncy. If we press our finger into one properly inflated, it's strong and resistant.

A person without signs of depression would act the same. Bouncy, strong, and resistant. The Morning Prayer poem I wrote symbolizes this type of feeling.

Morning Prayer

I woke up this morning so happy and gay,
glad to see another day.

As I opened my window to talk to the sun,
I found clouds in the sky having fun.

It was such a joy as I shaved
What a beautiful way to start the day.

Why aren't we more like creation
and heavens above
Being open with our love?

©Don Wooldridge

The Leaky Balloon

We all know if a little air leaks from the balloon, it's easy to push a finger into its surface and make a dent in it. We view the balloon as weak, with little resilience. But, it does still bounce back when you remove your finger. A person with mild depression would act this way, a little weary, distracted, and vulnerable, like the air was leaking out of them. I wrote this poem to describe what that "leaky balloon" feeling is like for me.

Nothing Rhymes

Today I'm not feeling so bold,
As I dream of a new life and cling to the old.

It's like floating down the shaft of a well,
Not even knowing that I fell.

Everything that I see,
Seems to be looking back at me.

Knowing that my heart is free,
Wondering how long before I'll flee.

To a new life, real and grand,
A little closer to the land.

In the still of the night,
I watch for the light.

As across my mind a new dream dashes,
And the beacon's light steadily flashes.

So, like a dying man,
I see everything for the last time.

Because I know that yesterday and tomorrow
Are never going to rhyme.
©Don Wooldridge

The Flat Balloon

Finally, there's the balloon with no air at all. It also has no strength, no resilience, and no way to recover. And here we find the clinically depressed person. Caused by physical disorders, beginning within the brain's makeup itself, the clinically depressed require help. Why? Just as a flat balloon without air can't get off the ground, neither can the clinically depressed person... without help from medical professionals, family, and friends.

The following poem, which I wrote during my divorce, is the best way I can depict this flat, clinically depressed feeling.

Just Me

*As I think of life and reflect back,
I wonder if I'll ever get on track.*

*Some days I'm up, some down, And
then I'm going 'round and 'round.*

*I'm tired of worry and headaches from fret,
But wherever I'm going I'm not there yet.*

*I've always wanted to be just me,
but it's been hard you see.*

*Through a past so heavy and hard to bear,
And all the pain I felt there.*

*So, I live with the yesterdays of sorrow,
searching for a new tomorrow.*

*Not knowing what I should do or be,
I'm stuck here today trying to be me.*

©Don Wooldridge

Now let's talk about how those of us who live with Bipolar disorder feel in our varying stages of depression. Those changes can be so much like the weather; let's look at it from that point of view.

Sunny:

Someone who looks firm and bouncy on the outside, is shining on the inside too. Very positive, a person in this state of mind is thinking "How Can I Help You?" Perhaps this poem can demonstrate the feeling.

When Breezes Play

Have you ever taken the time to watch the wind,
on a cool, cloudy day when everyone's in?
When there's no one to talk about or see,
she dances with the trees.
Running through fields of grain,
she combs a wavy mane.
Then, riding through the city behind a cloud,
she teases the windows 'til they rattle aloud.
She knows that a cool, cloudy day,
is her only time to play.
For tomorrow, when the sun is on the trees,
she'll have to be a gentle summer breeze.

©Don Wooldridge

<u>Cloudy:</u>

Someone who has felt weary, distracted, and vulnerable is self-centered and protective on the inside. When you ask this person to volunteer and help with one of your projects, you'll hear things like: "I'd like to help you, but . . ."

This type of person is hurting, focused inward on their personal concerns. They'll say, "Don't worry about me, I'll get over it."

And they will . . . eventually. This example is a mild depression, lasting a while perhaps, but allowing the person to "bounce back" like our description of the soft balloon. The poem on the next page is the way I depicted the feeling that I could "bounce back."

Winds of the Mind

Like a thunderstorm moving across the prairie,
dark clouds roll through my mind.

Thoughts explode like thunder,
dashing down in torrents like rain.

I am soaked with thoughts,
too numerous to be sorted.

Visions of life and death pass by,
the pain and suffering makes me cry.

And memories, both
sweet and sad.

There's been laughter, crying,
moments both confusing and painful.

But they say this storm will pass,
alas, when our loved ones pass.

©Don Wooldridge

Stormy:

Someone experiencing a deep stage of depression often feels threatened. The reaction to these painful feelings is to withdraw and protect oneself for hours, days or even weeks. It's a very dark and scary place to find yourself.

My doors would be closed. I could be covered by a blanket. The room could be dark. The withdrawal is so severe that even family members cannot extend enough feelings of comfort or safety to lead a person from withdrawal back into reality. Clinical depression is what this stage is called, and the only way to get the person out of withdrawal and back to reality is with the help of a qualified physician.

Bipolar II Depression:

Then, there's the person who has very little control of their moods and find themselves traversing this entire pattern of depression with regularity. This is what has been typical of my life with Bipolar disorder. Afflicted with a malfunctioning brain, I find no resting place in any of the stages of depression described above. Instead, I continuously move through highs and lows. My life consists of moving from sunny to stormy to cloudy, yet never staying in one place for long. For me, happiness is fleeting, and only passes by from time to time. I never know when it's coming, and never know when it's leaving. Perhaps the following poem that you read earlier in this book will shed light on the feeling.

<u>Going Sailing</u>

Inside my shell I feel like hell,
and my soul is dying.

As I contemplate life, death,
laughing and crying.

From day to day feelings vary,
and are mostly temporary.

But I wrestle with life, wondering why
people would rather live than die.

Is death like being drunk?
Slowly falling, lightly sailing,
kneeling to the ground with a thump!

Death doesn't seem that bad to me,
I think that is where I want to be.
©Don Wooldridge

May I conclude that depression does not, and cannot fit one definition? Although I've given you some examples of what it means to me, depression never looks or feels the same to all people. Depression is normal when it is resilient and short lived, like the cloudy stage. However, depression can also become serious and rob the sunshine and hope from people. Instead of being with people in the natural course of humanity, the depressed person withdraws and views the world from behind a screen. Awareness, understanding, and empathy - each required for those experiencing clinical depression who are relegated to viewing the world through a cloud of confusion and pain.

Even though I must face the Bipolar demons of my life's journey, I am becoming ever more passionate about how we can help those dealing with depression. I walk in their shoes and I can attest to the fact that there are simple things you can do to make a difference.

If you recognize someone who is going through the normal ups and downs of life, it would help most if you would quit asking what's wrong and simply provide a little cocoon of comfort and support until the depression goes away. Have a cup of tea with them. Take their kids away for a while. Help chauffer the kids, too. Go to the park, sit on a bench, and get them outdoors for a while. Exercise is very good, so get them up and take a walk.

However, if you see signs of a "flat balloon," like dark rooms, dirty dishes, clothes laying on the floor of each room and the laundry not done . . . these as serious signs. If the person is dressed in their robe and slippers when you visit in the middle of the day, there's another sign. If you see any signs that the person is avoiding contact with the world, or normal daily duties then it's time to get a physician involved.

There are psychologists and psychiatrists that counsel Bipolar sufferers, and teach them to recognize symptoms of depression, and suggest actions to take to minimize its effect. There are also medications available today that can protect a person from these dives into deep depression, and help those who suffer to create more resiliencies in their moods.

I wish we were all the same, then we would have only one definition for depression.

Depression has always been the major issue of my Bipolar disorder—the elephant in my room. It took some time for my doctor and I to find the anti-depressant that worked for me. Isn't it interesting that there isn't one mood stabilizer or one anti-depressant that works for everyone across the board?

What a relief it was when I finally had some control of my depression, and had some resilience; I was finally the image of the full balloon I described.

Escaping Stress Again

2000

SEPARATING MYSELF FROM Shawn by working in the clubhouse office relieved the depression, constant tension and interruptions that annoyed me in his building. Only because we both had a great respect for each other was I able to get away with it. Neither of us gave up on our positions about the busing issue, but we carried on together with other matters. The conflict was finally resolved by none other than the corporate office.

The V.P. of Operations, Shawn and the human resources manager met to discuss the expansion of my risk management and training function to include the whole 8000 acre property. In so doing, I was to report to the human resources manager. It was a decision that made it possible for Shawn and me to relieve the tension between us. (Though to this day he still reminds me that it was a big mistake to leave his agronomy department.) Time softens some things, but, at the time I couldn't pack up and move fast enough. I wanted as far away from that busing project as I could get. My new responsibilities included thirty-six buildings on the property. The six championship golf courses designed and built by Jack Nicklaus required five golf shops, six restaurants, a spa, and all the housekeeping, engineering, and agronomy facilities needed to provide the services members expected. I also assumed responsibility for the workmen's compensation insurance plan for the club, a foreign responsibility for me, but one where I made the greatest impact.

I developed a new type of relationship with my new boss. While I could depend on Shawn to back me up, even when I got out on a limb or in trouble, my new boss had tremendous political skills. Of course, I had none, or at least the one's I possessed were usually misused. Willingly, he suggested that he be the front man on all political issues so I could concentrate on managing the technical issues. It developed into a great partnership.

When I assumed responsibility for worker's compensation claims, our insurance rating was as least a 1.2 rating. This meant the club had to pay at least 20 percent more than the average premium. After implementing some controls for worker's compensation claims, our rating was reduced to a 0.6 rating, and we received a refund check for $28,000 and reduced premiums for the next year.

Of course, this was accomplished just by having someone investigate every claim. Employees didn't like that. I enforced the drug testing. Everyone was cautious. And, I denied some employee claims, alerting both employees and supervisors.

While other HR employees drove company vehicles I used golf carts or work carts in order to travel the back roads where I saw the hourly employees. Having the ability to speak Spanish allowed me to connect with them; they often gave me tips about unsafe equipment or activities. Keeping these anonymous allowed our relationships to continue. As the problems the workers recognized were solved with increasing frequency, they felt more comfortable stopping me and sharing other safety concerns.

Personally, I embraced my new position. I was positive, enthusiastic, and motivated by my successes. I was on a roll. An achievement I'm most proud of was the development of a property-wide fire evacuation plan for all 36 buildings on the whole property. It included primary and secondary evacuation routes, emergency containers at key intersections with vests, light sticks, and emergency supplies. When the plan was submitted to the local Fire Chief, not only did he approve our plan but he used his copy as a model for other HOA's to develop their own emergency action plans.

What a job! I can choose where I want to work—in the office or out in the field. I've got the undying support of my boss, plus Shawn when I need him to back me up. My wife's happy working here as well, and everybody loves her. I could do this until I retire!

SHOCKING

2002

———•———

I WAS 58 years old and in my fourth year as Risk and Training Manager for Desert Mountain Golf Club. The job offered a broad range of responsibilities, one of which was monitoring safety issues at a member outdoor party. In a stable, optimistic state of mind I answered a phone call from my boss, shortly after noon.

"Don," he asked, "are you still on the property?" "Yes."

"I'm in the office," he said, "When you can I'd like you to come by to see me."

Arriving at his office a few minutes later, nothing about his demeanor seemed unusual until he handed me a document to read.

"Don, what you're reading has been approved by our vice

president of operations, the controller, and myself. It requires you to make a decision today if it is to be effective."

That's a strange request. Why does he seem nervous?

He remained quiet while I read the document informing me that my job was eliminated and my employment at the club terminated immediately. Severance pay was included, but only if I signed a declaration to not sue or file an EEOC claim.

Stunned, I look up and asked, "Are you serious? Today is my last day?"

"I'm afraid so. It's nothing personal, Don. All department managers are required to reduce staff. I'm sorry your job had to be eliminated."

In shock, I look at my boss and remember all the stories he told me about the EEOC claims that he beat in court, saving his employers lots of money. I looked into his eyes and can see that he's worried about winning my age discrimination suit, if I should file one. An odd feeling surfaced; there is something about his presence that makes it apparent to me that by not signing this document, he and I will most certainly be in for a long, ugly court battle. I'm also confident the controller, who had somehow forced my boss into this position, will lie, cheat, and even shred evidence to ensure I lose the case. After all, only a few months earlier the controller had tried to discredit me in a meeting with the company President, but failed. Sitting there before my boss I concluded that a lawsuit would take longer than it did to divorce my wife, and the feelings in the end would be the same—hatred.

I signed the document, to his relief, then walked to my car and drove home on autopilot. I was numb. My brain seemed frozen. Arriving home I handed the document to my wife saying, "you won't believe what happened today."

"What's this," she asked.

"That, my dear, is justification for eliminating my job. As of today, I'm unemployed."

The next morning I began to worry. First, there is the unfair embarrassment my wife will have to bear working at the same club and fielding the "What happened to Don?" questions. Second is the question whether or not a 58-year-old man can find a job. Finally, how am I going to get out of this depression?

Numb and immobilized, I sat pondering what had happened and what to do. Fearing a deep depression that would last a long time, I vowed that it just couldn't happen without a fight, or I'd never find a job. So, I increased my antidepressant by 20 mg., then left a message for Dr. Mason

I was also realistic. At my age I anticipated a long job hunt. A serious depression that could last for months wasn't going to help me win a job. I had to get out of the house, and do something to manage my mood. The first thing I did was to contact a friend, Greg, who managed a local golf course maintenance department. I met him months earlier doing volunteer work at the Sunshine Acres Children's Home. Not expecting him to give me a job, I simply asked if he knew of

any job opportunities he might have heard about. He offered to call if he heard of any.

Then, in the middle of this tragedy we found a reason to smile, when my wife came home from work beaming. She finally got the company truck she'd been asking for to do her uniform deliveries.

Ohhh, was I suspicious. "What kind of truck is it?" "A Chevy S-10."

"What's the license number?" I asked, anticipating the answer.

"Oh, I don't know. WK something, I think."

I jumped out of my chair "You can't be serious! They just gave you my truck! I've only been gone one day!"

"I didn't know. Shawn promised me he'd find me a truck."

"And it doesn't bother you that they eliminated my job and gave you my a truck?"

"Oh, you know Shawn. He probably did it so he'd always have a good laugh about the situation."

We knew he would enjoy that prank, and we had a laugh together about the irony.

The second day I threw myself into all aspects of a job search that I'd learned during my years as a personnel manager. Utilizing the Internet for the first time, which is uncommon for my age group. I was able to remain in the moment, even when I was expecting depression to take over my emotions. Surprisingly it didn't. Maybe the new dosage was helping.

The third day Greg called and told me he had an approved requisition for a spray technician. Although he could only pay $8 per hour, he'd let me take all the time off I needed for job interviews.

Success! Work has always been vitally important to me. Getting outside and working physically every day helps fight against the depressive cycle that could have built up while sitting home all day.

Fighting depression is very difficult. But it's especially hard to do when I'm feeling passive. This is the time when I need a rescue dog who recognizes I am depressed, grabs my leash, and drags me outside for a walk. Wouldn't that be nice? The best therapy I can do to keep my mind off my troubles is physical work outside.

Nine months passed without a hint of a job opportunity. It felt like a lifetime. My mood was up when I was at work, but tanked whenever I focused on finding a job. It seemed impossible. Then I received a call from Memphis, Tennessee, and the corporate office of TruGreen LandCare, a landscape company. Based upon my Internet application they wanted me to interview at their Phoenix branch office.

Preparing to meet the local branch manager was a challenge for me. My spirits and energy were both very low.

Forcing a smile on my face I walked into his office.

But, I wasn't there long. He was brief and direct, offering me a job as their pesticide applicator for $10 per hour. I accepted on the spot.

My mood changed from survival to revival. Finally, a chance to recover from my devastating loss. On my way home I stopped by the golf course to tell Greg I had a job and would have to quit. Then I shared the good news with my wife.

Less than a week later the phone rang. My wife answered, told me it was the landscape company, and handed me the phone. It was the branch manager who had hired me.

"I'm really sorry that I have to say this, Don," he said, "But I have to rescind our job offer. I can no longer put you on the payroll."

"What?" I said in disbelief. "I thought you wanted me to start Monday."

"I know, and I'm sorry," he said. "But we've lost a major account. That means it's not possible to add anyone to our payroll. In fact, I may have to lay off someone else. I'm terribly sorry, but I have no other choice."

He's got no other choice? What about me? I don't have another chance. Look how long it took me to get just one interview!

My emotions sank. My energy tanked. I was devastated and just dragged myself around the house in a dark cloud of depression. In spite of my Bipolar medication, I was lifeless. I saw no hope. Where could I go? What more could I do? His call seemed fatal.

I felt like I was crawling on my knees when I went back to Longbow Golf Course to see Greg about getting my job back. It was a blessing to learn he hadn't turned in my termination papers yet, and I could just go back to work as if nothing happened.

Wow, what a lucky break! I was afraid I'd be sitting around the house wallowing in depression.

Still feeling the sting of being dumped, over the next week I worked my way back out of the negative mood I was feeling.

Who would want to work for a company like that anyway?

Just a week later my wife handed me a note with the TruGreen branch manager's name and number on it.

"He called a couple hours ago," she said, "and wants you to call him as soon as possible."

"Really?" I replied. "Why would I want to talk to him again?"

"I think you should," she said. "He sounded anxious to speak to you."

Reluctantly, I dialed his number, wondering what I was getting into. When he answered he was happy and positive, which made me very cautious.

"I am so happy you called back, Don. I have some good news for both of us."

"I don't understand what's changed," I said.

"I lost an area supervisor today, leaving a position open. I felt so bad about rescinding my job offer to you, but now I can offer you an even better job. It's a salary position that will pay you twice as much as my first offer. Plus, you'll have a company vehicle. You may start as soon as you want to. Tomorrow would be great."

"Are you serious?" I asked. "I don't even know what the job is."

"Tell you what," he said. "Come in early tomorrow morning and I'll fill you in and introduce you to the man you'll be replacing. I'm sure you'll like the job."

"Okay. I'll stop by the golf course and tell Greg what's happening, then drive over to your branch."

"Excellent. See you in the morning."

Do I really want to work with this guy? Off again, then on again. I'm not so sure.

We met the next day, and I was surprised at how much better the salary and benefits were compared to the job he had offered before. This seemed like a real blessing, since he offered the same pay and benefits as I had at Desert Mountain when they eliminated my job. I accepted the offer and started the next day.

Chaos

2003

THE ONLY PERSON my age at the landscape company was the man I was to replace. Five other area supervisors surrounded the desk we shared, in the corner of a "bull pen" office arrangement. I wasn't prepared for the chaotic start of each day.

First thing every morning at least a dozen Hispanic crew leaders filled the room, all talking at once in English and Spanish, getting their instructions for the day from their supervisors. During the day combative interplay occurred among the area supervisors, two or three radios played different stations, and sales people and clerical staff came and went at random. It was nerve racking for me. I wanted to scream. I couldn't concentrate on a thing. It was just as unnerving as the day I packed up and left Shawn's office at Desert Mountain. My best defense was to pick up my work for the day, get in my truck, and drive to a nearby park to work in peace and quiet. Two hours a day in the office was all I could stand.

My orientation to the new job felt like visiting a historical site. The man I was replacing didn't know how to use a computer, so he did everything on paper, stored in five boxes. He kept two stacks on the seat of his truck when he visited his clients' sites. They included his client lists and open work orders.

I was frustrated and wanted to burn them all and start over. The confusion and clutter was unnerving. To survive I had to take control. Creating a vision of how I wanted to do my job, I devoted every waking moment to make that vision come true.

I dove in with energy and enthusiasm, and spent weekends converting all the information into computer files. Similar to the way I attacked the insurance business, I pursued a vision of my landscape business. Enthusiasm became hypomanic as I compiled files of all customer transactions, then photographic displays of all desert plants and trees that could be offered to customers. I was going to carry only one laptop computer with everything I needed to conduct my business. It was going to be great!

As I recall this period of time, it's reminiscent of my behavior as an insurance agent for Prudential, where my magnificent plans were stolen from me.

Stepping back here and reflecting on my behavior for a moment, I'm seeing a pattern where I fail to adapt to the norm, and manically rush to create a new norm that I own. The drive to do so might come from hypomanic symptoms like inflated self-esteem or a feeling of grandiosity. Also it's not unusual to have a flight of ideas or to experience racing thoughts and increased goal-directed activity. Whatever the stimulus, the results appear very similar to my past behavior.

From time to time I observed supervisors, in the office, recruiting crew leaders from other supervisors by promising prime work sites or better pay. I hadn't lost anyone yet, but my two crew leaders were among the best the company had. I needed to do something to keep them and protect my business.

Still on a hypomanic roll, I vowed to protect myself. So, I introduced my crew leaders to an incentive plan that I created, hoping to reward them and keep them from leaving me. I paid my crew leaders the same commission I got for improvement projects they turned in to me. It could be things like irrigation repairs, replacing dead shrubs, removing or trimming trees. When I was paid, they were paid their commission.

It worked like a charm, although other area supervisors complained directly to the branch manager, and talked behind my back. But since it wasn't against company policy, I ignored them; I had a job to do.

Confident, arrogant, steadfastly independent… all traits of my hypomanic moods. I feel that I know it all and can do it all, in spite of company policy or anyone around me. And I'm good at what I do. However, I also alienate people.

One co-worker went so far as to sabotage one of my properties. At 7 AM one morning I reached the large office complex on Central Avenue of Phoenix, Arizona to walk the property with my crew leader. Immediately we noticed the flower beds bordering the main entrance had two feet of standing water. Before I could take any action the building maintenance manager approached me.

"You think this is bad," he said frantically, "you should see the basement. It's flooded."

Immediately my mind scanned the possibilities. It would be normal to think of a broken water line, or perhaps a broken clock would cause a problem like this. Logic told me to check the clock first. I found that someone had deliberately opened the box and set the two main entrance planter sprinklers to water continuously 24 hours a day. Assuming the clock was set at sundown, then the system ran for 12 continuous hours.

Given its location, hidden behind a wall in a clump of trees, there was only one person beside myself who knew where to find that clock, and that man was recently fired. This used to be his property, and he's the one who showed me how to find the irrigation clock.

He got his revenge, leaving me to explain to the irate property manager that the damage was caused by sabotage. I also reported the incident to the branch manager, who said that without physical evidence nothing could be done, but to tell the customer the company will pay for the damages.

In spite of these day-to-day conflicts I found some joy in the job, focusing on my clients and supporting my crews.

We were happy and productive, until the TruGreen corporation stepped in. It began with meetings led by the regional manager from California. There were handouts. There were procedures. The employee compensation system was being changed. We were shown a chart of skills our employees must demonstrate to attain a certain hourly wage. And it was my job to conduct the employee skill tests for my employees. The bottom line? Every employee's pay would be in jeopardy.

I took this change personally. My whole method of operating was threatened and I'd have to start over. The thought of redoing my operating style was depressing.

When I discussed the plan with my crew leaders, their response was, "Why should we take a test for our money? We'll just go down the road and work for another company."

The constant dreariness of depression I felt, made it hard to work. Most days I'd drive around my properties or go to the park and sit in my truck doing routine paperwork. I remembered that years ago I had been involved in a plan like this. It had failed miserably and created an employee backlash that lasted a long time. *Now, I'll be losing the productive team I have developed. I'll be forced to dig myself out of a big hole with inexperienced employees.*

Mulling all of the negative variables in my head, I couldn't picture myself doing this again. And I can't visualize a solution. I search for direction but my mind just goes in circles like it's stuck in neutral. So I give up. How can I possibly participate in what I foresee will be a disaster. To avoid the issue I'll announce my retirement to get away as fast as I can. After all, I'm 62 years old, which is early retirement age. No one will question it.

Perhaps this was the same visionary thing that happened to me at Manpower and Clark Equipment? Then again, perhaps it's just a manic response to losing control of my destiny.

Did I see something others didn't? It's unclear. However, in the end this corporate intervention was damaging. It resulted in area supervisors quitting, employees taking jobs with other landscape company's, and the two previously profitable branch offices in Phoenix being combined into one. All hopes and dreams for expansion into a third branch went down the drain. I escaped in time, and focused my attention on the pesticide licensing business I'd started in 2004.

BAD BUSINESS

2004

———◆———

I TESTED FOR and earned an Arizona pesticide applicator's license back in 1992, my second year working for Desert Mountain. Then, four years later in 1996 I earned my certificate in Golf Course Turf Management from Rutgers University and took the exams for the Arizona "qualifying party" license. This one required very technical knowledge and allowed me to authorize a business to purchase, store and apply pesticides.

Later, in 2004 I applied for and received a business license for Q.P. Services, Inc. This set of three licenses allowed me to hire, train, and supervise pesticide applicators.

After leaving TruGreen in 2006 I needed to grow the business. Besides adding three more clients, I became actively involved in the state pesticide regulatory commission meetings. When I learned that new certification tests were being developed, an idea sprang up. The more I thought about it the more exciting it became.

Here is an opportunity to go back to the exciting work I love. Designing interactive courses designed to train pesticide technicians to pass the state tests.

That's all it took to start a hypomanic mood. I pursued the idea every waking hour. My constant energy helped me form plans and actions to make this idea a reality. I thought the plan was brilliant and unmatched. It was invincible!

As I write this memoir, I'm starting to see a pattern developing. Just as I mentioned when I began work with TruGreen LandCare. It's like I hone in on the North Star and follow it. Only instead of a star… it's an idea, an opportunity, or a chance to control my destiny.

Pursuing my latest vision, I stumbled across a company in Tucson, Arizona that had interactive training software and servers accessible from anywhere in the country. Here's my opportunity, I thought. After some meetings and an initial payment, I had all the software to develop training programs for pesticide applicators. I could see people studying for state tests at home on their own time. What a win-win. They save time and money, and I collect a fee from every user.

A local pesticide supplier supported what I was doing and gave me some of his courses to format on this new delivery system. I submitted these new online training courses to the state agency and received approval to offer them to the industry, giving participants the same training credits that they would receive in the classroom.

The software company was impressed with my work. The local supplier saw many uses for my courses. I was on cloud nine. I had a winner, and a two year exclusive contract for the state of Arizona. I was riding high, just like hypomanic states of mind when everything fits together like a glove. The super-energy pulls me up higher and higher, just like a roller coaster crawls up to the peak before the fall.

I was so excited that before I rolled out the programs in Arizona, I wanted to expand the same concept to the state of California, where opportunities were much greater. Through a vendor, I was introduced to an innovative business owner who wanted me to convert his courses to my online training system.

I was very enthusiastic and proud of myself. I'd found something I just loved to do, and it had the potential to be an excellent retirement business. However, in spite of my efforts and the support of others, the idea didn't pay off for reasons I never anticipated in my unrealistic enthusiasm.

First, the culture of the pesticide industry didn't embrace the idea. Workers wanted the eight hour day off work for their training. Secondly, computers in business offices were too old to run my sophisticated software. And, finally, most pesticide applicators didn't know how to use a computer.

Consequently, I didn't have enough business to stay open, and discontinued the service.

I crashed emotionally as yet another bright Don Wooldridge idea failed. It would prove to be the third time hypomania has pulled me into business ventures where I was unaware and unprepared for the real world.

All it takes is a quick mood shift and I'm grabbing onto a new concept—my mind begins whirling as I create all sorts of possibilities. Each contact and each new brilliant idea drives my enthusiasm higher. Taking existing information, creatively reshaping it to fit a unique delivery system, and offering it across the country drove me on. You'd think I'd learn, but I just don't seem to be able to pass up the seductive allure of creativity.

Some say that I have created training programs before their time. That may be true, but it's obvious I can't run a business. The combination of my personality and mood swings makes it impossible to be consistent, and I suspect that's what it takes to create and run a business. I finally learned not to invest in my grand ideas.

It's been an expensive and difficult lesson to learn. I currently contract a literary specialist to manage all of the business and communications associated with my novels. I only do the creative work today. Anything that requires a business skill or consistency I stay 'hands-off.' I ask myself, "Would you trust a Bipolar person to run your business?" I'm confident that I've learned the answer is 'No.' But the lesson was learned too late!

You Need Help!

2006

———◆———

MY WIFE BEGAN sending signals (more like road flares) that we had to do something about my behavior. My moods were changing abruptly. I was extremely irritable, going into outbursts about little things, and using poor judgment about what to say and when to say things. I even managed to offend one of her family members, and damaged our relationship.

Oops! What's going on?

Immediately, I started looking through our insurance provider's list of psychiatrists. There were many, but I've learned not all of them have experience dealing with Bipolar patients. I chose doctors close to us, then called the insurance provider and asked if their practice included bipolar patients. I took the names of three who did and called their offices, asking how many years they had been treating manic-depression. The response I felt most comfortable with was from Dr. Mason, so I made an appointment.

I entered his office with a list of questions, determined to verify his qualifications. Serious thoughts prevailed… *I've had numerous doctors and I don't want one doing his training on me. I'm the one needing help.*

Imagine my surprise when Dr. Mason told me to sit down, he had some questions for me. I was taken aback.

"Don," he asked, "Have you ever had a DUI?" "No sir," I answered.

"Have you ever been in jail?"

"No,"

"How about drugs? Have you used drugs?"

I wonder where this was going. I'll answer his questions, but how far is he taking this?

"Never have used drugs." I answered.

"How about sex? Have you ever frequented prostitutes?"

"No, I haven't. But I don't understand why you're asking me these questions."

"Well, Don," he said, "It's not uncommon for a person with Bipolar disorder to have experienced one or all of these conditions. I'm really surprised, with your illness, that you've managed to avoid all of these difficulties. The fact that you have none of these in your history of Bipolar illness is simply amazing. It is extremely uncommon."

For this reason, Dr. Mason determined that my illness was actually Bipolar Type II, with a less aggressive and less extreme form of mania called hypomania. While that may be true, I would discover that less aggressive and less extreme doesn't actually mean less troublesome.

He also discussed self-medicating techniques used by Bipolar patients. The first was alcohol to calm excitement or anxiety. The other was smoking, also a calming and relaxing drug. As we talked about my history and doctors he was surprised when I mentioned Dr. Dunstone, my doctor in Kalamazoo, Michigan.

"I used to live in Kalamazoo, Don."

"Really?"

"Yes, and I knew Dr. Dunstone well. We worked together when I was President of the area Psychiatric Association. Actually, I think he's retired now."

"Wow! That's an incredible coincidence," I said.

I had no further need to ask my questions. I felt this was the doctor for me, and little did I know that our relationship was going to be journey of discovery. I left his office with a prescription for a new anti-depressant and orders for a blood test for a lithium level (Blood test details were described previously in Chapter: Lithium 1973).

FINALLY—INSIGHT

2007

———◆———

ONE PROBLEM I'VE always had is failure to more fully understand my Bipolar disorder. Now, many years later, I'm finally finding ways to understand what's been happening to me all my life.

Always looking for the spike of mania and the crash of depression defined by Bipolar I, I never saw this happening in my life. Confused, I thought I was blind to the phenomenon. My life was one of constant changes, not peaks and valleys.

From my understanding of the brain's nervous system, a simplified way of explaining it is analogous to the battery in your car. A car battery is made of cells containing plates. There is an air space between each plate so they do not touch and short out. Electrolyte fluid fills up the space between the plates. Current flowing from one plate to the other passes through this liquid electrolyte.

I was surprised to learn that the nerve endings in the brain don't touch each other, just like battery plates. Just imagine the nerve endings in the brain as the plates in your battery, and the fluid connections between nerves as the electrolyte in your battery. Now you've got a simple picture of how the nervous system sends messages through the brain. However, if there are not enough chemicals in the brain to conduct electrical signals, then the brain malfunctions, just like a dead battery.

A person with Bipolar behavior doesn't always have the necessary chemicals to complete the nerve connections properly. When chemical levels are sufficient, everything is okay. However, when stress creates increasing levels of cortisol, and light fluctuation affects melatonin levels, the brain may not function properly.

While this information makes sense to me, I could not translate it into my life of constantly changing moods, until I found an article developed by Drs. Dean Mackinnon and Ron Pies, which they published in April 2006 through PsychEducation.org.[20]

_____

[20] PsychEducation.org, Rapid Cycling and Mixed States as "Waves" April 2006

The descriptions that follow are from their article on "affective instability".[21] This term means, roughly, unstable mood and energy.

"People with such instability have big changes in their mood, energy, or creativity over time. They may have easy tearfulness, such as crying over a commercial on TV. They may have extreme episodes of anger, often over a minor event. They can sometimes have inappropriate "mirth"—laughing too loud or too long, or being too giddy or goofy."

Drs. Mackinnon and Pies offered a new explanation for this instability, in the three steps that follow. Their 2006 model is quite different from the current diagnostic system for Bipolar disorder.

In their article, (which by-the-way has graphs I can't print here) Drs. Mackinnon and Pies say: "You see, according to the current official rules of diagnosis the DSM[22] (Diagnostic and Statistical Manual of Mental Disorders)

---

[21] MacKinnon DF, Pies R. Affective instability as rapid cycling: theoretical and clinical implications for borderline personality and Bipolar spectrum disorders. Bipolar Discord 2006: 8: 1–14. [a] Blackwell Munksgaard, 2006

[22] Def'n; DSM, Diagnostic and Statistical Manual of Mental Disorders

'mixed states' include only phases of full manic and full depressive symptoms.

The idea that these can occur together may be news to you. Similarly, those same rules only allow cycles as short as four days. Any shorter doesn't fit on the DSM map.

"But patients *do* have other combinations of depression and hypomania, or mania—not just the two worst phases together. And they *do* have cycles shorter than four days. The DSM can't really handle these variations . . .when I show our graphs to my patients, I often see the 'light bulb' go on in their head."[24]

It certainly did for me when I saw them. Finally, a picture of how I feel. It was as if I had drawn the chart myself.

(see charts at PsychEducation.org, Rapid Cycling and Mixed States as "Waves," April 2006.)

"Using a model, they explain how symptoms shift over time in a way that seems a lot closer to what some people

---

24   MacKinnon DF, Pies R. Affective instability as rapid cycling: theoretical and clinical implications for borderline personality and Bipolar spectrum disorders. Bipolar Discord 2006: 8: 1–14. ª Blackwell Munksgaard, 2006

live through than the typical stories about Bipolar disorder—you know, the ones that talk about 'manic episodes' as though they were completely separate phases followed by relatively normal functioning." [25]

Always believing, for years and years after my diagnosis, I should be having these completely separate phases, and never observing them, this concept of symptom shifts hits home for me.

Their article continues, "For a lot of people, there are no phases of normal functioning (or very brief ones); instead, many people have only symptoms, varying from one kind to another." [26]

That's exactly how I feel. Constantly varying symptoms that see normal functioning only as they pass by to the next symptom.

---

[25] MacKinnon DF, Pies R. Affective instability as rapid cycling: theoretical and clinical implications for borderline personality and Bipolar spectrum disorders. Bipolar Discord 2006: 8: 1–14. [a] Blackwell Munksgaard, 2006

<u>STEP ONE:</u> SYMPTOMS VARY SEPARATELY FROM ONE ANOTHER & AT DIFFERENT RATES

One element is mood, another is energy, and a third is intellect (speed of thought, creativity, and the ability to connect ideas). If they all go up together—and far enough 'up'—this would be what is commonly called a manic or hypomanic episode,

I've been at this hypomanic state. It's those times when my creativity is high, I'm on cloud nine, being in the scene with my characters as I write like mad. I have so much energy that it may be three hours before I stop writing, only to grab a snack, and dive right in again.

If mood, energy and intellect, all come down together, far enough, that would be an episode of 'major depression'." [26]

---

[26] MacKinnon DF, Pies R. Affective instability as rapid cycling: theoretical and clinical implications for borderline personality and Bipolar spectrum disorders. Bipolar Discord 2006: 8: 1–14. [a] Blackwell Munksgaard, 2006

I've been here also, when nothing seems possible or worthwhile. Just getting out of a chair takes special effort. The despair and sense of immobility leads to hopelessness, then thoughts of suicide.

"But now," the doctors say in their article, "we can see how 'agitated depression' could be part of a Bipolar problem, when the energy curve is up while the others are down."

I have found this to be an explosive state of mind. I get furious if interrupted. Though I have no proof, I suspect this is the state I'm in when I go into a rage. It all stems from my need to be alone, to concentrate on my internal thoughts, to deal with the anger I feel. To make any demand of me is very disruptive, no matter how small you might think it is.

Moving on, they say, "An unusual combination usually recognized only on inpatient psychiatry units, when a person is agitated yet hardly moves, a so-called 'manic stupor'. But imagine what a milder version of this would look like: a woman perhaps who would know she needed to get moving, indeed she would be thinking of many things she needed to be doing, and she might really want (in a very powerful way) to be doing them, and yet her body would refuse to go along. She would be lying there on the couch, miserable yet not really depressed, wondering what was wrong with her and why she couldn't get herself going."[27]

---

[27] MacKinnon DF, Pies R. Affective instability as rapid cycling: theoretical and clinical implications for borderline personality and Bipolar spectrum disorders. Bipolar Discord 2006: 8: 1–14. [a] Blackwell Munksgaard, 2006

I'm in this state of mind now. I have thoughts every day about losing weight by lowering the sugar in my diet. Also exercising in the gym, on my bike, or just walking. Like the description of 'manic stupor' above, I just can't make myself get up and do it. Even if I were standing right by the gym, I wouldn't go inside. I'd look through the window and tell myself I should be in there exercising, but I wouldn't.

My emotions have been at a plateau for many days now. I'm not hypomanic, and I'm not severely depressed, although I feel like I could be depressed. Instead, I'm functional at home and in public, but without much feeling, energy or enthusiasm.

When I'm in this state of mind my internal thoughts are negative. Like this example:

My wife hates "top lights" as she calls them. Like a miner, she lives with only one light on. Personally, I am affected by S.A.D. (Seasonal Affective Disorder) and I've gotta have light! Sitting in my Laz-Y-Boy chair, these thoughts go through my mind.

Let's have some light!

I hate a grey house.

I hate her.

I shouldn't have married her. Now I have to live the rest of my life in a dark house.

I hate a dark house.

That's not going to happen. I'll spend $2000 if I have to, and have the biggest sky light installed in the ceiling, and she won't be able to turn it off!

Then I get up, turn on a light switch, sit back down and forget the whole thing.

"Another very important combination psychiatrists see commonly: the energy wave is up, but the mood wave is down. In this case, the timing is such that the intellect wave is up too, but not as high as the energy—yet there are *many* combinations. This could be called 'dysphoric mania': energized, as in a usual manic phase, but mood is very negative."[28]

---

[28]

MacKinnon DF, Pies R. Affective instability as rapid cycling: theoretical and clinical implications for borderline personality and Bipolar spectrum disorders. Bipolar Discord 2006: 8: 1–14. [a] Blackwell Munksgaard, 2006

STEP TWO: THE WAVES CAN COME AT NEARLY ANY SPEED.

The doctors' article continues. "This might seem fairly logical and it certainly matches my experience with patients, but it doesn't match the official rules of diagnosis: <u>Bipolar disorder is supposed to have phases lasting at least 4 days</u>.

Shorter than that, and it doesn't fit the official DSM model. But the shorter versions are seen so often they have their own names, say doctors Mackinnon and Pies."[29]

"Now one would have to admit that when the 'cycles' get so short there are multiple moods in a day, the condition gets hard to distinguish from 'normal emotions'—normal reactions to events that last a few minutes or even close to an hour or so. Yet this ultra-ultra-rapid cycling ('ultradian') is quite commonly seen in kids who have Bipolar disorder, where it can be so extreme as to be clearly recognizable as 'not a normal emotional reaction'."

29

MacKinnon DF, Pies R. Affective instability as rapid cycling: theoretical and clinical implications for borderline personality and Bipolar spectrum disorders. Bipolar Discord 2006: 8: 1–14. [a] Blackwell Munksgaard, 2006

STEP THREE: How waves lead to continuous and continously varying symptoms

Doctors McKinnon and Pies combine the first two steps to reach the most important implications of this third step.

The manic, depressed, and mixed cycles are often seen as neat, smooth waves, but reality seems to be even more unpredictable: the waves have long humps sometimes, and short humps at others; and long troughs, or short troughs, as well. Many people with Bipolar II do not have the 'well shaped intervals' in between periods of having symptoms that are often spoken of in websites and books about Bipolar I. This leaves them somewhat puzzled. Do they really have 'Bipolar disorder?' Why? They never really have 'episodes' let alone "manic" episodes. Yet rapid cycling of the individual symptoms, <u>at different rates</u>, can create a varying pattern of <u>nearly continuous symptoms</u>. Instead of having identifiable 'episodes', this person has almost constantly shifting symptom phases that blend into one another."[30]

Note: Drs. Mackinnon and Pies' article includes numerous other ideas, built around these wave diagrams.

---

[30] MacKinnon DF, Pies R. Affective instability as rapid cycling: theoretical and clinical implications for borderline personality and Bipolar spectrum disorders. Bipolar Discord 2006: 8: 1-14. Blackwell Munksgaard, 2006

That's it! Continuous symptoms! I have to agree. My Bipolar behavior is always moving, unpredictable and never static. My life is like a beach ball floating in the bay.

Today I'll be floating squarely in front of the beautiful city skyline.

Tomorrow, I'll be off to the side, looking at the city from a forty-five degree angle.

Day three I'll have moved again and be viewing the city from a ninety-degree angle.

If you happen to see me on the first day, floating out in the bay, the next time I'm just not going to be in the same place. Each day you must search if you wish to find me.

It's this constant change and inconsistency that causes the surprising feedback about behavior that I'm not aware of at the time. I want discipline, but my brain isn't the same every day! I've heard it said if you do anything for 21 days, it becomes a habit. Geez, I've never done the same thing for 21 hours in my life! I have wanted to, very strongly so, in fact, many times in my life. Like reading the Bible every day... exercising every day... dieting and losing weight.. but it never happens. Why? Because the emotional pull of the Bipolar illness changes faster than 21 days. There's the euphoric energy, creativity, and excitement that makes a diet seem dull. Then, there's the icky, sticky low down feelings that make everything seem impossible.

I want consistency, but my brain doesn't focus on details, or procedures.

Let's say for example that my wife and I are driving to a church across town.

She would say, "Let's give them a call for directions before we leave."

I pause a second, view the map in my brain, confirm it, and say "Don't worry about it, I know the way." And I do! I just follow the visual map stored in my head from the last time we made this drive (like a GPS). However, along the way my wife will ask if I remember the minister's wife's name.

"What? I don't even remember the minister's name." "What's the matter with you?" she would say. "They were at your parent's 50th wedding anniversary just last month! Surely you could remember his name." "Sorry, but I can't."

That's left-brain stuff you see, remembering names, details, and procedures. I'm good at the exciting, colorful, visual stuff. Cameras? Don't need them. I can store unlimited pictures of people, places, and things up there in that right brain compartment. Plus, it's a lot more exciting than details and procedures!

There are periods of time when it is easy for me to visualize, anticipate, see, sense, and describe things that are only vaguely familiar to me.

During those times I also experience heightened productivity, and become extremely insightful and creative. Doctors say that more often, however, comes the distorted thinking and impaired judgment that are Bipolar characteristics.

Of course, these periods of being extremely insightful, with distorted thinking and impaired judgment has the effect of alienating or distancing family, friends, and associates.

Because of this constantly changing behavior that doctors MacKinnon and Pies described in this chapter, fear has been my co-pilot every day since 1973, and it's growing larger, despite my passion and commitment to share my story with you. Fear falls over me like a dark, heavy cloud; I wonder how you'll view this memoir.

A-FIB

2008

EARLY IN 2008 I experienced periods of weakness, fatigue, and difficulty breathing. Every time I did something physical, I needed a nap. I mentioned this at the cardiology clinic during a routine appointment, and the physician's assistant put me through a series of tests that revealed I had atrial fibrillation (A-Fib).

Many times I would feel a very fast vibration in my chest, and it concerned me. I'd make a beeline to the cardiology clinic and tell the desk clerk I thought I had a heart incident going on. Without an appointment, the PA and nurse would find a place to conduct an ECG, and document the A-Fib incident.

A few days later, I was driving on the freeway and had contractions across my chest, giving me the sensation of a belt tightening around me. As I slowed to pull off the road, I felt the constriction diminish and finally went away; when I proceeded, the contractions eventually returned. I drove directly to the cardiology clinic where the nurse did another ECG test.

On another occasion my chest felt like I had a humming bird trying to get out every three or four seconds. Very strong thumps in my chest, like someone was punching me. Again, I headed for the cardiology clinic to be tested. I had to laugh when the PA said I was one of the most sensitive men she'd ever known.

If only she knew the truth.

My treatment began with medication. None of the first three prescriptions worked well, and the fourth one put me in the hospital's ER department with a pulse of 30. Nurses were surprised I could walk and talk with a pulse so low.

May of 2008, after my subsequent release from the ER, my electrocardiologist scheduled surgery to cut a laser maze on the outside of my heart's atrium, via the De Vinci Robot. The resulting scars create little motes that break up the path of random electrical pulses in the heart.

While waiting for that to happen, my psychiatrist shared an FDA notice that the anti-depressant I take could cause atrial fibrillation if my nominal dosage of 40 mg was exceeded. Even though I'd been taking anti-depressants for thirty years, this new information didn't provide a clear answer for me, since atrial fibrillation was common in my family. My grandmother had it, and suffered many strokes that eventually caused her death. My mother suffered from A-fib also, but refused to acknowledge it. I suppose that's why I never gave it much thought until my series of ECG tests.

I do have strong opinions about having a heart condition, however. I've spent so many years dealing with Bipolar II behavior that I can't imagine wanting to live another thirty years with it. It would be like carrying a rattlesnake in my pocket, knowing it will bite me, and always wondering when it will happen.

That is why I will do whatever is necessary to keep my Bipolar behavior under control first, in spite of A-fib. Missteps in behavior hurt me more that heart problems. My erratic behavior is just as punishing to me as any life-threatening condition. Death because of a heart problem could serve to eliminate all of my emotional tension and turmoil.

My psychiatrist had me continue my anti-depressant protocol as I prepared for surgery. The procedure went well, and I spent only two days in ICU for observation. In September of that year, my electrocardiologist scheduled a catheter procedure to block a circular loop obstructing electrical signals from the upper heart to the lower part of my heart. The result; control of the A-Fib condition and renewed energy without the need for heart medication.

I couldn't hide from my cardiologist though. He'd been watching my tests and activities behind the scenes. During a 2009 follow-up visit, he asked if I had taken the sleep test he prescribed before my surgeries. Of course, with all the pre-surgical stuff going on, I hadn't. He wouldn't waver from his request and set up the test for me. He felt the sleep test had to be done, because sleep apnea can contribute significantly to the A-Fib condition I experienced.

Of course, with all the pre-surgical stuff going on, I hadn't. He wouldn't waver from his request and set up the test for me. He felt the sleep test had to be done, because sleep apnea can contribute significantly to the A-Fib condition I experienced.

Come to think of it, my psychiatrist has told me that sleep patterns also have a huge impact on mood disorders. I wonder, will this test show any effects on my Bipolar II disorder?

I reported for the first of two overnight sleep tests. On the first night a nurse monitored my sleep, and recorded how often I snored or stopped breathing. I guess I didn't do so well because I stopped breathing 56 times in an hour. This verified the doctor's suspicion that sleep apnea might contribute to erratic heart rhythms. When the brain notices I've stopped breathing it orders a shot of adrenalin to restart the heart. The adrenalin goes to both the heart and the brain, jolting the heart back into action. However, if this occurs between heartbeats a new rhythm can be created that is out-of-sync with the body.

Thus, atrial fibrillation starts and blood flow reduces and can pool in the heart.

The second night of testing determined the setting for my sleep apnea machine.

Thinking back on all the discussions about my medication, I found it interesting now to find I was adding yet another health issue to my list: sleep problems. Early on, my sleep pattern was a priority that Dr. Mason and I monitored to determine my anti-depressant dosage. He told me that change in sleep patterns signal a changing mood.

And here I am, using a breathing machine to get my sleep pattern under control.

This all fit with what I experienced with great frequency: when I'm hypomanic, I have trouble getting to sleep; yet when I'm depressed I have trouble waking up.

I received my C-Pap machine and began sleeping through the night. My mood changes were farther apart, and Dr. Mason was pleased that I had a more predictable sleep pattern. The more predictable sleep patterns have reduced my mood swings and depressive cycles.

Triggers

2009

———— • ————

IN 2006 DOCTORS McDevitt and Wilbur[31] wrote, "A trigger is an environmental, biological, or situational factor that causes symptoms of Bipolar disorder to begin. Some common triggers are lack of sleep, high levels of stress, the change of seasons, inconsistent patterns of eating, skipping medications, and changes in normal patterns of exercise, among others. Your ability to link symptoms to environmental triggers will be the key to managing your Bipolar disorder. Exercise increases cognitive functioning, fights depression, and improves overall mental health"

About May 1st, when the winter season transitions into spring, I can inadvertently take too much anti-depressant for the light exposure of the longer days.

---

[31]   Bipolar 101, A Practical Guide; 2009 Ruth C. White, PH.D., MPH, MSW and John D. Preston, PSY.D., ABPP

There are times when I lay down to sleep and my arms just won't calm down! I feel an annoying, constant tingling from my shoulders to my wrists.

Hoping I can make it stop, I use a stretch band to exercise my arms, When this happens I realize it's time to reduce my dosage of anti-depressant by 20 mg for the summer season.

Conversely, when fall comes around October 1st, this lower dosage will result in my mood getting flatter and flatter. After the slightest activity I collapse on the couch for a two-hour nap. In this zombie-like depression I just go through the motions with no energy. Life can return to normal when I increase my anti-depressant by 20 mg. to my winter dosage. My mood picks up again.

It's taken about 32 years to learn these things, and I am grateful for the knowledge, because regular sleep and the seasonal adjustment of my anti-depressant dosage has helped my mood swings. They don't seem to change as frequently. Other triggers that it took years to learn about include:

1. *There are times when I notice I have a slow memory, like not remembering the name of a friend's wife, the name of the local university, the brand of my neighbor's car, and the like. Just real simple day-to-day things that we take for granted. When this happens it's a clue that I'm tired and need more sleep. If I have trouble sleeping, I am happy to know I can be proactive and lower my antidepressant dosage.*

2. *Another trigger that helps me manage my moods is noticing high carbohydrate cravings. It's a clue that my mood is changing and my antidepressant dosage could be too low. When this mood hits me I'm constantly hungry, eating something every hour. If the refrigerator is bare, I'll go out to find something.*

3. *I drink alcohol more frequently as well. Though I am conscience I should not be doing this, I ignore the facts and follow my impulse.*

4. *My energy level is revealing as well. Some days I'll have so much energy that I can trim our shrubs, wash the car and then take a ten mile bicycle ride. Other days I'll confine myself to the house, sitting in my favorite chair for hours watching movie after movie on TV.*

I stay in constant touch with my psychiatrist to ensure he's in agreement whenever I make antidepressant dosage changes.

Even though I'm taking the proper dosage of lithium, I can still become hypomanic. Lithium just minimizes the intensity. When I'm hypomanic for a period-of-time, and have a need to calm down, I'll drink alcohol. Alcohol is a depressant, of course, and that's exactly what I want.

Luckily, if I overdo it, I'm a sleepy drunk instead of becoming mean, wild, or crazy.

Smoking is another way of self-medicating. Taking quiet time to smoke is calming and relaxing.

When I smoke, I prefer a pipe, which is therapeutic and calming while I get in touch with my thoughts.

Not good habits since it's been documented that alcohol can trigger depression, while the use of caffeine or tobacco, can trigger mania.

LIGHT AND SEASONAL CHANGES

2009

———•———

Though I've never been diagnosed with Seasonal Affective Disorder, (S.A.D.) I'm extremely sensitive to light. Or, I should say, the lack of light. I don't mind rain, but the dull gray skies that come with it depress me. A dark house makes me feel claustrophobic, and depresses my mood. I believe that's why I did so well working outdoors maintaining golf courses and landscapes in Arizona. There was lots of light. Even now, as I write I need to stop and get outdoors. People I know want to turn lights off to either save electricity or reduce heat in their home. I just shake my head. I've never seen a light I didn't want to turn on. This sensitivity to light impacts the way I manage my medication.

One important management tool for Bipolar II disorder is controlling light exposure. Here's what the Harvard Medical School has to say about light and why it's so important.

"Light at night is bad for your health, and exposure to blue light emitted by electronics and energy-efficient light bulbs may be especially so."

"Until the advent of artificial lighting, the sun was the major source of lighting, and people spent their evenings in (relative) darkness. Now, in much of the world, evenings are illuminated, and we take our easy access to all those lumens pretty much for granted."

"But we may be paying a price for basking in all that light. At night, light throws the body's biological clock—the circadian rhythm—out of whack. Sleep suffers. Worse, research shows that it *may* contribute to the causation of cancer, diabetes, heart disease, and obesity."

"But not all colors of light have the same effect. Blue wavelengths—which are beneficial during daylight hours because they boost attention, reaction times, and mood—seem to be the most disruptive at night. And the proliferation of electronics with screens, as well as energy-efficient lighting, is increasing our exposure to blue wavelengths, especially after sundown."[34]

34

http://www.health.harvard.edu/newsletters/harvard_health_letter/201
2/may/blue-light-has-a-dark-side/

The response to seasonal changes works so well for me, I had to seek out the reason why. I was curious about this relationship with light. What I found was an answer both broad and deep. I began at psycheducation.org website and found this statement.

"More of this drama has yet to unfold. But we are watching one of the greatest medical detective stories ever: we are watching the discovery of the mechanism of Bipolar disorder, which turns out to be much more complicated than was thought 10 years ago. Why, back then most of us were still waiting for the discovery of a single gene that might be "the cause." Wow, was that ever wrong. We're seeing that Bipolar disorder is a problem in the operation of very normal, standard cellular processes—like sleep, and response to light.[35]

"Alert, Alert: watch out for one kind of light at night. Recent research has shown that one particular kind of light is the key to regulating the biological clock: blue light (blue wavelengths of the light spectrum)."

Researchers in Berlin, Germany had this to say about blue light. "Another important study showed that blocking blue

---

[35] http://www.psycheducation.org/depression/BlueLight.htm

light at night really does change brain chemistry, just as one would hope. Here's how that was done. Melatonin, a hormone associated with falling asleep, is decreased by light. That fact is very well established. What's new is that you can prevent this reduction of melatonin by blocking blue light with a simple pair of glasses made to block that particular color of light.[36]

"Now researchers are finding increasingly that an out-of-phase circadian rhythm is a health hazard. 'Maintaining synchronized circadian rhythms is important to health and well-being,' says Dieter Kunz, director of the Sleep Research and Clinical Chronobiology Research Group at Charité–Universitätsmedizin Berlin.

"A growing body of evidence suggests that a desynchronization of circadian rhythms may play a role in various tumoral diseases, diabetes, obesity, and depression."

Wow, I can relate to this. I look back on my many years in the training and personnel recruiting business and it opens my eyes. Traveling across different time zones was upsetting my circadian rhythm; impacting my Bipolar moods.

---

[36] Summary of light therapy by David C. Holzman @ http://www.ncbi.nlm.nih.gov/pmc/articles/PMC2831986/?tool=pmcentrez

My overseas travel obviously had an even worse effect on my Bipolar II behavior. Recalling the stress in my marriage, and the difficulty I had sleeping tells me that at that time of my life I was doing all the wrong things for maintenance of my Bipolar illness.

The research continues, "In other experiments, blue light also proved more powerful in elevating body temperature and heart rate and in reducing sleepiness, according to Gilles Vandewalle, of the Center for the Study of Sleep and of Biological Rhythms at the University of Montréal. In experiments published in the September 2003 issue of *The Journal of Clinical Endocrinology and Metabolism,* Brainard, Czeisler, and Steven Lockley."

I'm sure the tension and stress I felt while working in the consulting business led to an elevated heart rate and high body temperature. That might explain why I sweat so profusely while working there. Even worse, and adding to my fatigue, is the fact that I had sleep-apnea. So, during those years of hypomania, depression, stress and fatigue, I suffered from irregular sleep patterns. And, a critical recommendation to manage Bipolar disorder is a regular daily sleep pattern.

Fortunately, my sleep has improved greatly since I began using a C-PAP machine at night. And, my mood shifts have been more subdued and less frequent. Just think, this all started with a racing heart beat called atrial fibrillation. I guess everything happens for a reason.

"Alfred J. Lewy, M.D., PH.D, now director of the Sleep and Mood Disorders Laboratory at Oregon Health & Science University, suggested that "humans might have seasonal rhythms cued to natural photoperiod," which he says would be insensitive to indoor lighting.

"The bottom line: blue light is a powerful signal telling your brain "it's morning time, wake up!" Although not formally tested yet, it looks like the last thing you'd want to be doing right before bed is looking at a blue light. Uh, oh. You can see it coming, can't you: what color is the light from your television? How about from the computer screen you stare at (after 9 pm)?

"The good news is this: you might be able to significantly regulate your Bipolar cycling, and at least find it easier to go to sleep at night (without medications like zolpidem (Ambien), lorazepam (Ativan), trazodone, etc.), by avoiding blue light at night. So, here's the treatment recommendation doctors ought to be giving you . . . no TV or computer after 9 pm if you're going to bed at 10 or 11. End the TV/computer even earlier if you go to bed earlier.

I've had quite a few patients tell me this step alone really helped them." [37]

"The irony of blue as an environmental agent is that before the industrial age, it was merely a color. The unnatural lighting conditions we created turned it into both a potential hazard and a treatment for the ailments it brought about. In addition to the traditional architectural values of visual comfort, aesthetics, and energy efficiency, Brainard says architectural lighting must be redesigned to account for its biological and behavioral impact on humans. *George C. Brainard, director of the Light Research Program at Jefferson Medical College of Thomas Jefferson University.*"[38]

How lucky I was to make such a drastic career change and get out of office buildings, taxicabs, and airports where blue light prevails. By working outdoors eight hours a day in the natural sunlight my moods stabilized and my energy level was consistent.

Unconsciencely I had reduced blue light significantly and added physical exercise to my day, both positive steps in managing Bipolar disorder. It would be 20 more years before I came to understand how significant this was to my mental health.

---

[37] http://www.psycheducation.org/depression/BlueLight.htm

[38] http://www.psycheducation.org/depression/BlueLight.htm

Based on my experience with seasonal changes in medication, I've learned to apply the effects of light and seasonal changes to personal travel. For example, when we travel to the Midwest for family visits, the light exposure there is much less than it is in Arizona, where I'm at my lower summer dosage. Before we travel north, I'll increase my anti- depressant to my normal winter dosage, about five days before our trip in order to build the anti-depressant in my system.

Since I started adjusting my dosage, I have very few depressive responses while in the new and darker climate. Any depression I do have rebounds quickly without those around me noticing.

It's amazing to me what a simple dosage adjustment can do. I guess you would say I am fortunate these adjustments work and I can depend on them whenever I travel.

For years I was a slave to my Bipolar condition. All I knew was how to react to my changing moods. It's such a blessing to learn there are ways to be proactive, and minimize the effects of my brain disorder. Managing light exposure and responding to seasonal changes have been a tremendous help for me, and has minimized the Bipolar mood changes.

STILL SOLO

2010

———•———

MY WIFE IS a woman of many questions. As I made adjustments to my Bipolar medications she'd ask what I was doing, and if my doctor approved. Over time I took this to mean she had an interest in my Bipolar issues and treatment. After getting permission from my psychiatrist to bring her to one of my sessions, I invited her to come along.

"I forgot about it," she'd say, "I'm busy. Maybe next month?"

The next month I reminded her, again. "Do I really have to go? After all, what am I going to learn that I don't already know."

I didn't give up inviting her. I was so hopeful that this would be the beginning of a partnership that would help her understand my behavior and how to deal with it. Finally, we were in the car and going to my appointment together.

In the doctor's office I sat back and let the doctor and my wife communicate without me interrupting. This gave me a chance to observe my wife's reaction to the discussion.

I was shocked by what I observed. Her responses were bland, with literally no emotion, and she asked no questions, which was totally out of character.

I went cold, although not as devastated as the time when my first wife walked out on my psychiatrist. After all, I've been in this alone for years. Now I had to face the disappointment I was feeling. Was it too much to have such high hopes that we could work together—perhaps giving me some support and reprieve from this constant self-analysis?

But it's not all about me. Why wouldn't she behave as she did? Bipolar personalities are not attractive. And I have empathy for my wife and those loved ones who must be on guard for the ways a Bipolar personality can impact their daily lives. So, it's reasonable to conclude that someone, even a loved one, would not enthusiastically join their Bipolar companion on a journey down the deep dark alley of unknowns, where Bipolar demons cause erratic mood changes.

LOVED ONE'S ROLE

2010

———— ✦ ————

I'VE THOUGHT A lot about what my wife goes through. I'm not only empathetic with her role, but view it as similar to having a new pet thrust into her hands every day. For example:

Let's say on the first day a little puppy is delivered to her by the animal shelter. Throughout the day she would experiment and learn the puppy's behavior, potty habits, feeding and sleeping habits. At the end of the day she'd have a good idea what she's dealing with.

Then, the second day, the animal shelter takes that puppy away and gives her a new one. Throughout the day she experiments again and learns the puppy's behavior, potty habits, feeding and sleeping habits. At the end of the day she, understands what she's dealing with concerning this new puppy.

On the third day, the animal shelter takes the second puppy away and gives her a third new one. Throughout the day she experiments and grows accustomed to the puppy's behavior, potty habits, feeding and sleeping habits. At the end of the day she's confident she knows how to deal with this new puppy. It is not reasonable to expect any person to take lightly this "every day is a new puppy" kind of experience.

Well, in my wife's life, she can expect me to be that new puppy! Even though she doesn't know from day to day when the mood change will occur, it's always expected.

As the puppy in this scenario, I don't know what to expect of myself either. I can go to bed moody, and wake up light and bright. The opposite can be true as well. I can be irritable, sarcastic, and chip away at everything my wife says or does throughout the day.

On any given day, my wife has to figure out how I'm behaving in order to determine how she's going to take care of herself. Does she feel comfortable around me in the house? Or, does she need to avoid me by leaving to shop and run errands?

After our visit to my psychiatrist, I've lost any hope of someone coming helping me understand and manage my illness. The responsibility for understanding and dealing with my Bipolar condition is solely mine.

CREATIVITY

2011

———• •———

THINKING MY HEART troubles were behind me, I felt blessed. Life was good, so I bought a semi-recumbent bicycle to ride for exercise. I felt like a new man and rode it over 1800 miles during the year. That is until I began getting weak and tired, again. As I recall, I would work outside, or ride my bike for two hours, and then collapse from fatigue.

Is it natural, or even acceptable that a nap becomes routine?

My first thought was that I was depressed and my anti-depressant dosage was too low. Immediately I visited my psychiatrist, and he suggested I see my cardiologist before we made any dosage change. The cardiologist's exam revealed I had a weak pulse of only 45 beats per minute. My doctor scheduled surgery to implant a pacemaker.

Before the surgery I jokingly said to a couple of my friends, "I wonder what I'll be like when I finally get some blood to my head." Secretly I wondered if my low pulse was having an effect on my Bipolar symptoms. With that in mind, during post-op recovery I asked the electro-cardiologist who performed the surgery if he could set the speed of my pulse.

"Of course," he said. "The pacemaker will keep your pulse to a minimum of 70 bpm. You should have nothing to worry about."

While recovering from surgery my mind exploded with ideas! Mentally I had new energy, and the urge to write was surprising, and became real. I visualized the story just like I'd watch a movie. I knew it from beginning to end. I wrote like mad. I had a natural passion to finish a project, which I'd never done before. Concerned I had gone into a hypomanic mood, I was wary of the possibility.

I'll have to wait and watch to confirm it!

I guess I answered my own question about getting blood to my brain. All the creativity I'd known in the past burst out anew. I finished a Christian workbook about Proverbs for teenagers called *Rules To Live By*. I found a Christian publisher I thought would help me through all the stages of publishing process. Hooray! I was published.

If I'd been hypomanic, as I suspected, the events that followed would have deflated me quickly. The first blow came as a reaction to the cover, when a major independent bookstore buyer recoiled at the picture of a male referee. She informed me that only boys would be interested, then expressed disappointed that it wasn't a sports story.

The second blow occurred when I gave the book to an acquaintance at a faith-based children's home. An ordained minister, he informed me the book would not be welcome in churches and Bible studies because it hadn't been written by a person trained and ordained by a church.

The fact that my work was of no use to the public didn't drive me into a deep depression, like disappointment and failure frequently does to me. Instead, for some reason, I just kept plugging away at writing. I was encouraged that there was no change in my attitude or mood. Secretly I hoped that getting my heart condition stabilized and more blood to my brain might have cured my Bipolar disorder.

I kept writing. Ideas filled my brain constantly, and my next attempt received such negative feedback I didn't even spend money to publish it. Then a story appeared in my mind contrasting small towns with big cities, and the bartering that I'd seen in those small towns pitted against the I.R.S. I liked the idea. I didn't need credentials to write a fictional story. I decided to try it.

The writing came easily. I was filled with imagination, creativity, and an intensity that made me self-absorbed. I'd see the setting in my mind with all the characters in place. I visualized scenes filled with people and then heard the conversations between characters. I could visualize the whole town, knowing who was where, doing what, and so on. It was wonderful, except that it revealed one glaring problem—interruptions.

I'd have a picture of a scene and action in my mind like a movie when my wife would open the door to my office.

"I'm leaving now. If Shirley calls would you please tell her I'll come by at two o'clock? Bye."

I boiled with anger. Doesn't she realize what she just did to me? In less than a minute she completely collapsed the visual picture I had in my head. Now my imagination is blank and I've lost everything. I am frustrated at the thought of taking half an hour just rebuild it, knowing it'll never be the same as it was. All those feelings—they just won't be there... the dialogue I wanted won't be there.

She just ruined everything!

My anger isn't really the other person's fault. I'm frustrated and angry that I lost the image and have to rebuild it. As a way to minimize this type of interruption, I've tried to find remote locations to write. I've rented cabins at the state parks for two or three days at a time, allowing me solitude to focus and write without interruption. It's just another mechanism to help me deal with my emotions when in a hypomanic, self- absorbed state of mind.

I could blame all my self-absorption on hypomania, but I have to be fair—I've done the same thing when I'm depressed. In those moments when life bears down on me and I find myself cuddled up in a cocoon of misery, I don't want to be bothered either. My doctor continues to remind me that not all things are a result of Bipolar because my personality still plays a role in my behavior.

This is so new to me I don't know how to differentiate my behavior between personality and Bipolar. Every new insight takes time and practice to build some sort of confidence.

MAKING COMMITMENTS

2012

———— • ————

ONE THING I can't adjust for is a future commitment. I didn't know this until I was asked to sing a solo at our chorus performance. I chose to sing "The Quest" from *Man From La Mancha*. I knew it well, having practiced it with a voice coach, and felt confident. I could easily sing it three weeks later for a crowd of 200 people.

I saw no reason to doubt myself the night of the performance, until I began to sing. Oh my God, what was wrong! I barely remembered enough words to start the first stanza, but couldn't remember the rest. The same thing happened with the second stanza. I drove the pianist nuts. Not until I got to the third stanza did I find solid ground and sing the song successfully.

I was embarrassed and depressed. I never sang "The Quest" this poorly. After some analysis on my part, I came to the conclusion that a mood shift had affected me. In an "up" mood when I made the commitment, my mood had changed completely when it was time to perform. Since I hadn't experienced this type of change before, I couldn't anticipate it. The effect on me was huge! The shock of realizing my mood changed between making the commitment and the performance clearly opened my eyes.

What a fool. How could I have missed this? I should have known.

I vowed to never forget this lesson, and only commit to something within the next day or two. Any longer time frame and I will have to decline, because it's too risky for me.

New Avenues of Feedback

2013

———— • ————

VOICE

Driving across town toward home I remembered an errand I could do on the way. I called home, but there was no answer, so I left a message.

"Pat, I have to make an extra stop on the way home, so I'll be thirty minutes later than I planned."

When I arrived home, my wife still wasn't there, so I checked to see if my message recorded. As I listened to it I thought, Holy cow! Was my depression ever apparent! Just the sound of my voice and the speaking pace—everything signaled depression.

A few weeks later I got a new cell phone and recorded a greeting. When I called a friend in Montana, there was no answer. So, I left a message. When she called back I couldn't answer, so she left this shocking voice mail for me:

"Listen, I've got to tell you that if I didn't know you, I'd never call you back. Your voice sounds so gruff and sinister it's scary. That can't be you. Please change it. I don't like that guy."

Because I deal with a lot of uncertainty, these two incidents have become tremendous aids for me. The fact that my mood came across in phone messages was very exciting. This is the first time in my life I've had a way to identify my mood. I've been guessing all my life.

Now, when I think my mood's changed, I can leave a message, and then listen to it.

WRITING

Sensing my mental state while writing fiction novels surprised me. It wasn't the intensity that surprised me, but the longevity. Being hypomanic in the past would typically last only a week or two. In the case of my novels it lasted for months. I could write for three hours straight without noticing the time. I'd go to bed, lay my head back on the pillow, and begin to hear characters' conversations. They were good. I didn't want to lose the thought, so I'd get up at 9:30 p.m. and write until midnight. As I wrote the story, I could feel myself as an extra person in the scene, observing and listening to each character's dialogue. I just couldn't let go until they stopped. I loved it.

Along the way my hypomania would come and go. It could have been simple enthusiasm. Then there would be days when I'd be tired, fatigued, or in a gloomy mood. I didn't know it until I started writing and learned that I could read the difference in my moods.

Unlike the euphoric and highly sensitized mood where I could feel myself in the scenes, my depressive moods resulted in prose that plodded along, uninspired, and flat.

Soon I began to understand, and used the difference in mood to decide whether to spend my time writing creatively, or to pursue the more mundane task of editing and proofreading. It was a revelation.

Epiphany

2014

The Lord is my Shepherd I shall not want…[39]

I wonder, *Does the Lord's flock include black sheep?*

As a youth my behavior would bounce between good and bad like most ten years old boys. Though my parents insisted I go to church every Sunday, I resisted strongly.

Our Sunday church service required all of the children to sit in the sanctuary with our parents until the children's sermon was over. Then we left as a group for the Sunday school classrooms.

I hated Sunday school. Always trying to find a way out, one Sunday as we walked down the back stairs of the sanctuary to the Sunday school classrooms, I noticed a short hallway off to the right leading to a door.

---

[39] The Holy Bible, NIV, The book of Galatians

The next Sunday I hung to the back of the crowd. As everyone headed on to Sunday school class, I walked over and tried to open the door. Success, though I was skeptical when I peeked into the room and saw janitor supplies. Stepping into the room I heard someone talking. Standing still, I realized it was our preacher giving the sermon up in the sanctuary.

Wow, what a find! I closed the closet door and sat down to listen. When I heard the organ play and a rush of footsteps over my head it was time to go. I waited outside the closet for the Sunday school kids and blended into the crowd to meet mom and dad up in the lobby.

Mom ruffled my hair and asked, "Hey honey, how was Sunday school?"

"We learned a lot, Mom," I'd say as I shared parts of the preacher's sermon that I heard.

"How interesting," she said, "That's what our sermon was about, too."

My hideout served me well for most of the year, until the day Mom approached my Sunday school teacher.

"I just want you to know how much Don loves your class.
And he's learning so much, too."

The way he looked at me I just knew my cover was blown. "I find that quite interesting, Mrs. Wooldridge. You see, Don hasn't been in my class all year. Have you, Don?"

Embarrassed and angry with me, I thought Mom would eat me alive. Instead, she grabbed my ear, twisting it as she smiled at the teacher.

"Well now, I can take care of that."

"Donald Wayne Wooldridge," she said, dragging me along by my ear, "We need to talk."

Mischief was part of my DNA as a child. But as I look back I recognize signs and symptoms of my Bipolar disorder. Specifically my aversion to crowds, rules, regulations, processes, and procedures. I never grew out of it, because these are actually a part of my Bipolar II disorder. I didn't know this in 1973 when I was diagnosed as Bipolar, and only recognized it sometime after 2011.

Knowing that Bipolar II is a behavioral disorder, I've struggled with the issue of being a faithful Christian. I found in the Bible that the book of Galatians has a specific list of behaviors that helped me know when I was being a good or bad Christian.

The first part is Galatians 5:19-21, which states "the acts of the sinful nature are obvious: sexual immorality, impurity and debauchery; idolatry and witchcraft; hatred, discord, jealousy, fits of rage, selfish ambition, dissensions, factions and envy; drunkenness, orgies, and the like. I warn you, as I did before, that those who live like this will not inherit the kingdom of God."

On the other side of the coin is found in verses 22-25 of the book of Galatians. "The fruit of the Spirit is love, joy, peace, patience, kindness, goodness, faithfulness, gentleness, and self-control. Against such things there is no law."

While the message is clear, it disturbs me that I'll never measure up because of my Bipolar II disorder. As I wrote in Chapter 2006, my psychiatrist told me that sexual immorality, discord, fits of rage and drunkenness were common behaviors my illness doesn't allow me to control.

I'm just as disturbed by the love and goodness part of these verses. I feel love, joy and peace only when I'm in a hypomanic mood. And, I certainly don't feel patience, kindness, or goodness when I'm depressed. Plus, as I've said before, self-control goes out the window when I'm in a rage.

Since 1973 I've devoted my Bipolar life searching for stability. Something, just anything that I can count on. All I've found is change. My behavior will always wander between weak and strong, depending upon the mood shift I find myself in. It's disheartening to know I'll never be the husband I want to be; or the father I envisioned; or the kind of Christian my friends are. I was angry with God because I couldn't be these things.

Constantly I've wondered what my role in life is. If I'm so unpredictable I'll never be like the people I see around me, which always causes me to feel inadequate. I'd almost given up looking for an answer to this question when in 2006 I was asked to serve on a pastor selection committee for our Chapel.

Ongoing meetings and interviews brought us to the point of making our final selection. We asked each of our top three candidates to preach at one of our Sunday Chapel services. Afterward the committee selected our new pastor, on a five to one vote. Our decision severely disturbed the woman who voted "No."

Following my heart instead of my head, I worried about the woman who voted "No." I went to visit her that night. As we sat on her patio, we talked through her concerns, and I presented the majority case to her. I left confident that her concerns were alleviated. (I later learned that as soon as I left she called the pastor of our sponsoring church and urged him to come and resolve the matter. So much for democracy and diplomacy.)

What a surprise at chapel the next morning to see the minister of our sponsoring Baptist church standing at the pulpit addressing our congregation. His message was clear. His church sponsored our chapel. His church provided all of the clerical and financial services to us for free. Therefore, our satellite chapel was his responsibility, and as such he alone would assume the authority to select the succeeding pastor. It was totally inappropriate, he said, for us to form a committee and to select a pastor.

He informed us that he was personally appointing the pastor. We were duly reprimanded; the man happened to be the music director on his church staff.

I learned a lot about myself during this process. It was an epiphany to get the answer to my role in life? This process made it so clear. Elation welled up inside me and I felt a huge weight lift off my shoulders. I knew! I finally knew! I sat down immediately and wrote a poem to ensure I didn't forget the lesson, and named it "The Rower."

The Rower

I am what I am,
and, God made me a "Rower."
I'm big, strong willed, and there
when the captain jumps the sinking ship.
There are those who cry for help,
and those who fall on their knees to pray.
Instead, I grab an oar and start rowing,
until everyone realizes our boat isn't going to sink.
True to human nature, they complain,
about the direction the boat is going.
And I stop rowing,
waiting directions from God.

©Don Wooldridge

Finally, I understood my role in life. It is to jump into action to make things happen. Get things started. Then, like the rower, bow out and let someone else carry it through. I've been this way all my life and never recognized it, always a starter but never a finisher. It became clear that it's part of my personality. I needed to accept it, quit worrying about it, and move on.

This revelation allowed me to quit worrying about being perfect. I came to grips with the fact that God knows all about me. I accepted the fact that He knows I'm Bipolar II, and He's accepted me that way. In His greater wisdom maybe he will use me to make a difference in someone's life. Maybe in the lives of those who also suffer from Bipolar II. Perhaps in the lives of those whose hearts will be opened through awareness, empathy and acceptance. Maybe, just maybe, my story will help another person with Bipolar II disorder.

As a long-suffering Bipolar II patient, I'm grateful that I'm okay exactly the way He made me.

ABOUT THE AUTHOR

Don Wooldridge is an accomplished author in several genres; now retired, he draws on the writing skills amassed over 30 years in training and development as a technical writer, instructional and interactive learning systems designer and producer. Education enriched Don's life along the way; earning a teaching degree from Southwest Texas State University and a two-year certificate in Golf Course Turf Management from Rutgers University.

The author delivers a uniquely personal story; he suffered from Bipolar II disorder for over 40 years and still has episodes of the illness. *Fear Is My Co-Pilot* is the powerful, moving memoir of Don's life, from the moment he looked outside a hospital window, struggled with his scattered and broken thoughts, and pondered how it was that only yesterday he was a successful mid-level manager. He takes readers through myriad experiences of his life's duration as he learned to cope with the affliction. Don frankly discusses his inability to fully rid himself of overriding fears of being discovered by his friends and peers, and the incredibly difficult obstacles he overcame to become a highly respected professional. This powerfully delivered memoir is destined to become a classic in its genre.

OTHER BOOKS
BY THE AUTHOR

Don Wooldridge is a prolific writer, with many words to share in multiple genres. You can find his collective of works on his website: Don Wooldridge Author

http://donwooldridgeauthor.com/books-by-don-wooldridge/

OR

http://amzn.to/1ZMzLuW

REQUEST FOR REVIEWS

Authors come to the end of a book and naturally feel it is a product of beauty; the prose has been polished to perfection, and they have crafted a "masterpiece" in stolen moments, around an impossible life schedule. To ensure the reader experience is enhanced, authors commission a beguiling cover, and invest in a top editor and interior designer.

However, until a reader has spoken of that experience, its value remains unclear to other potential readers who count on honest, authentic reviews and feedback to impact their purchase decisions. Readers look for reviews written by their peers as a sort of social proof, and authors look to them to relate to their work from a reader's point of view, to shape how subsequent projects are approached.

With that in mind, I hope you enjoyed sharing my journey through life, managing as best I could the impact thrust upon me by an un-requested relationship with Bipolar II disorder.

Thank you in advance for taking the time to post a review for the book on Amazon; many readers will not take that step to purchase and read... until they know someone else has led the way.

If you enjoyed reading *Fear Is My Co-Pilot* I would appreciate it if you would help others enjoy the book, too.

LEND IT - This book is lending enabled, so please feel free to share with a friend.

RECOMMEND IT - Please help other readers find the book by recommending it to readers' groups, discussion boards, Goodreads, etc.

REVIEW IT - Please tell others why you liked this book by reviewing it on the site where you purchased it, on your favorite book site, or your own blog.

http://amzn.to/1ZMzLuW

EMAIL ME - I'd love to hear from you
booksbydon@gmail.com

NOTES

53553650R00166

Made in the USA
San Bernardino, CA
20 September 2017